ENJOY SWIMMING

Margaret A. Jarvis, M.C.S.P.

Former Senior Physical Education Adviser for Shropshire,
and Swimming Tutor at Loughborough College Summer School.
Advanced Teachers' Certificate of the Amateur Swimming Association.
Diploma and Service Cross of the Royal Life Saving Society.

Illustrations by R. Macgillivray

FABER & FABER
3 Queen Square, London

First published in 1972
by Faber and Faber Limited
3 Queen Square London WC1
Printed in Great Britain by
Latimer Trend & Co Ltd Plymouth

ISBN 0 571 09742 1

by the same author

YOUR BOOK OF SURVIVAL SWIMMING AND LIFESAVING
YOUR BOOK OF SWIMMING
YOUR BOOK OF DIVING
SWIMMING FOR TEACHERS AND YOUTH LEADERS
YOUR BOOK OF SWIMMING GAMES AND ACTIVITIES

ENJOY SWIMMING

Acknowledgements

The author wishes to express her thanks for helpful assistance to:

Beulah Gundling, Aquatic Artist, U.S.A.
Surgeon Captain Stanley Miles, R.N.
Miss L. R. Stephen, B.A., F.L.A. Reference Librarian; and Salop County Council Library.
Mrs. M. Bithell, M.A., F.L.A. Librarian, Chester College.
The British Museum.
Shropshire Schools photographed:
Apley Park, Bridgnorth; Albrighton County Junior; Haughton Hall, Shifnal; Royal National Institute for the Blind, Condover.

Thanks are due for permission to use photographs to:

London Express News and Feature Services for No. 1 (a).
The Associated Press Ltd. for No. 1 (b).
West Riding News Service for No. 2 (a).
West Midland Photo Service Ltd. for Nos. 2 (b), 4 (a) and (b), 5 (a) and (b).
The Guardian for No. 6 (a).
The Yorkshire Press Agency for No. 6 (b).
The Shropshire Star for Nos. 7, 8 (a) and (b).

TO MY THREE SISTERS ETHEL, DORA AND
VERA, WHO ALL KNOW HOW TO ENJOY
SWIMMING

> '*And we, along the table-land of beach blown*
> *Went gooseflesh from our shoulders to our knees*
> *And ran to catch the football, each to each thrown,*
> *In the soft and swirling music of the seas.*
>
> *So in we dived and louder than a gunshot*
> *Sea-water broke in fountains down the ear*
> *How cold the bathe, how chattering cold the drying,*
> *How welcoming the inland reeds appear.*'

EAST ANGLIA BATHE for John Betjeman,
but Mablethorpe and water polo for us!

From *Collected Poems*, published by
John Murray Ltd.

Contents

9

Illustrations

11

FIGURES

1 · Why

The first reason why I want to write this book is that I want to share the enjoyment that I and my family have always found in swimming. We were lucky. Our parents were both outstanding pioneers in the swimming world. My father, John Arthur Jarvis, was the first swimmer to win three individual Olympic Gold Medals in Paris in 1900, plus 108 swimming championships, and fourteen international water polo caps. He had a distinguished career as a demonstrator of the Life Saving Society's methods abroad, and saved seven people from drowning. We were delighted when, in 1968, his achievements were honoured at Florida's International Swimming Hall of Fame, which was founded to perpetuate the memory of famous swimmers, to provide a research centre for the sport and a meeting place for swimmers from all over the world. He was only the second English swimmer to be so honoured; Captain Webb, the pioneer Channel swimmer, being the first. My mother fought many a battle for mixed bathing, and for modifications in women's swimming costumes which would make racing possible. Subsequently she acted as team manager in Norway and at Empire and Olympic Games. My aunt, too, was the team manager of the first Women's Olympic team, in Stockholm in 1912.

It was almost inevitable, then, that my sisters and I should become competent swimmers. But what we remember most, and with gratitude, is that our parents never allowed swimming to become a thankless chore for us. Enjoyment came first, even in our competitive days, and our training in watermanship consisted of fun and games, interspersed with hard labour! This pleasant introduction has led to a lifetime of enjoying swimming. Today, some young swimmers almost wear themselves out training for competitions, but it is well worthwhile remembering that swimming for the majority is a leisure pursuit.

These are personal reasons; but there are, of course, countless other reasons why swimming is a most valuable recreation, as well as the most popular sport today. First, it is essential for personal safety, and should be the required passport to all other water sports. There are still far too many deaths from drowning each year. Secondly, it is one of the healthiest forms of exercise, and one of the few in which muscles can gain full strength and yet remain supple and undistorted. All muscle groups are used, and in most strokes they are used equally on both sides of the body. Swimming stimulates the circulation, promotes good ventilation of the lungs and develops neuro-muscular co-ordination. Unlike most other sports it can be exceedingly strenuous without profuse perspiration. It promotes habits of cleanliness, and stripping for swimming allows the sun and air to get to the body and removes feet from the restrictions of socks and shoes, so that they can feel the texture of tiles, grass, sand or pebbles. It develops personal confidence; individuals often have to overcome a real fear of the water, and as they progress they acquire a sense of self-reliance, and an increasing pleasure in their mastery of an element which is not a natural one for man. Certainly in today's rush and bustle swimming can play a part in providing relaxation and the easing of nervous strain.

Swimming has many practical advantages over most team sports. It is inexpensive, and requires very little uniform clothing or expensive equipment. It need not depend on elaborate organization or on good weather conditions. It should be possible all the year round, from early morning until late at night; alone, in a mixed party, or with a wide age group. It is one of the very few sports which can be enjoyed to a ripe old age, and coronary thrombosis is said to be less likely than with other sports. Swimming is not a commercial sport, in which a few participate, whilst the rest pay to watch. Galas are staged mainly for the benefit of the competitors and demonstrators, and the spectators are usually relatives, friends or erstwhile swimmers.

Swimming is one of the few forms of exercise which people with physical and mental handicaps can enjoy. Lord Byron, who was an expert swimmer, was crippled, but in 1810 he emulated Leander's swim across the Hellespont. The first swimming club specifically for the handicapped was founded in England in 1949, and the majority of its members were spastics. In 1952 the Association of Swimming Therapy was formed and held its first inter-club gala in 1955. It also provides lecture teams for overseas organizations. Swimming plays a large part in the rehabilitation of the injured, and at Stoke Mandeville Hospital swimming galas are held. Olympic Games for the disabled, in which swimming is one of the major sports, now follow on after the normal Olympic Games. A relay team of eight handicapped swimmers successfully crossed the Channel in fourteen hours. It is truly a wonderful sight to see pupils, minus their various aids, calipers and wheelchairs, enjoying their new-found freedom. Survival and other awards are successfully taken by handicapped swimmers. I know, for example, a sub-aqua instructor who has become a second-class diver himself, in spite of severe polio wastage. Able-bodied non-swimmers would surely set about learning to swim if they saw some handicapped swimmers, thoroughly enjoying the mobility, independence and dignity which water support gives to them. The boys in plate 2 (b) are blind and deaf.

The final reason why I presume to write another book on

swimming is because every year, as expert swimmers are produced at a much younger age, many are subjected to dull routine repetitions of activities, there is a greater danger of losing sight of the pleasures of swimming which could result in staleness and boredom. Even games can become monotonous if pursued too long, or are inappropriate for the age or ability of the group. Many activities can be quite pointless if there is no encouragement or coaching at the right moment, and if results are not checked. The young swimmers' potential should never be underestimated, and they should be stimulated by challenging and imaginative situations. Swimming is a 'cradle to the grave' sport, and people of any age can acquire and enjoy further skills in watermanship.

I hope that this book, which draws on my own experience, will give everyone reading it ideas, and starting points, from which to go forward and *Enjoy Swimming*.

2 · Who

FAMILY

Swimming is one of the few recreations in which all the family, including cousins, aunts, uncles and grandparents, can meet on almost equal terms and enjoy themselves together.

When a whole family swims together, the women, who can stand the cold more easily, usually stay in shallow water with the small children, while the males enjoy more active games in deeper water, but for a shorter time. Families who have swum together over the years always observe the elementary safety precautions. They know that a red flag means danger; they bathe from safe beaches; they do not plunge into unknown waters and they heed the advice of the 'locals'. They have due regard to the capabilities and sensitivities of each member. Boys are not teased if they get out of cold water before girls; no one staying close to the shore is called *chicken*; no one is singled out for all the ducking; a child is never seated on an adult's lap for a slide down a water chute into deep water (the adult's weight may take them both to the bottom, so that the child is fighting for breath).

Some swimming families enjoy surfing, water ski-ing or sub-aqua, whilst others prefer sailing and boating, but only good basic swimming will give the necessary peace of mind for enjoyment of such pursuits. Swimming, and the other water sports to which it may lead, can be valuable in the way they draw a family together for its leisure activities.

PARENTS

Parents who cannot swim themselves often do not insist on their children learning, and this becomes a vicious circle. The notes received in schools often show the prejudices against swimming: 'You are not to take John to the baths as he cannot swim.' 'Janet has a bath at home, so please excuse her from swimming.' These are extremes, but there are genuine fears of infection, or of irritation from the use of chlorine. Here one can only remind parents that the risk of catching a verruca is less dangerous than the risk of drowning, and that most pools now use a weaker solution of chlorine, and that chlorine goggles can be bought.

Other parents maintain that they have managed well enough without being able to swim. They may not realize how many new water sports are now available to everyone, and that they are either condemning their children to be non-participants, or putting them in danger, when, for example, they hire a boat or canoe. Non-swimming parents may also fail to recognize the attractions and dangers of water, and are unable to take the quick preventative action which may avert an emergency. A boy, I knew, dived into a river, swam across and rescued a baby, whilst the mother, who in the first instance need only have thrown herself on the ground and reached out to grab the child, stood petrified on the bank. This is the kind of situation in which a non-swimmer can unwittingly endanger others.

Today lack of opportunity cannot be an excuse as there are several ways of obtaining tuition. Age should not be a barrier, as people over eighty have learnt to swim, and only regretted that they had not learnt earlier, and so had missed years of enjoyment. Poor health can only be an excuse if the doctor agrees, as swimming usually promotes better health!

If you decide on private tuition contact the coach at the local pool. Individual coaching should ensure good progress, especially if you can choose a quiet time at the pool. You can enjoy your early lessons as a duck unobserved, and emerge as a swan ready for family admiration. Holiday camp and seaside pool lessons are usually available, and daily lessons achieve more rapid results than lessons once a week. 'Learn to Swim' classes for adults are organized by Local Education Authorities and the Central Council of Physical Recreation. Some of these are even arranged as residential courses. Many adults prefer learning to swim in a small class, which provides a sense of companionship and competition, and can be very helpful for nervous beginners. These adult learners often get the bit between their teeth, and progress to the Improvers Class; Survival; Life Saving and even Sub Aqua.

We still have far too many non-swimmers in this country. Parents cannot safely leave the teaching of swimming to the schools, as at least 300 children under fourteen years of age are drowned in Britain every year. Many schools are not able to give swimming lessons, as there are not sufficient pools available. My own personal experience, and that of nearly all children of keen swimming parents, was a very early and pleasurable introduction to the water. Whenever my parents went in I would hang on to their backs like a koala bear until I was swimming, and so water never held any terror for me.

INFANTS

Making friends with water starts in the home and not in the swimming pool. From the very first day, in the small plastic bath the baby should experience the feeling of little drops of water sprinkled and left on the face. Later a little shower with a sponge on the head should be given. When you think he is ready, probably between six and eighteen months, you can put him in the full-sized bath. There can be a small amount of water at first and the familiar floating toys should surround him. Extreme care must always be taken to give support under the head, because of its great weight in relation to the size of the rest of the body. Let him lie on his back for a short time. Repeat this every day, gradually increasing the water depth. Soon he will feel what it is like to be water-borne, but your hand will still give firm support under his head. This head support will only be decreased as he begins to manage his water balance and becomes relaxed in the water. At the toddling stage he is ready for real fun in the bath. He can push himself about balanced on his hands with only his face out of the water, both on the front and back. He can use the inclined end of the bath as a water chute, and with a well-soaped seat, or tummy, slide down it. Never wipe his face dry, as it is important that he should get used to it being wet. Children progress individually, so go at the child's own pace with water enjoyment as the aim. Never compare his progress with a sister, brother or other child, but be prepared to hasten slowly. The regular daily dips will ensure long-term results, if you are patient. This is also the time to train the child not to foul the water. Visits to the local paddling pool will add confidence. The child should lie down in the pool as well as walk about in it.

It is a natural reaction to close the eyes under water so start early by letting him look for, and pick up, large plastic coloured pegs from the bath bottom. Be sure to count them before and after in case he thinks they are edible rewards! He can also imitate your breathing out through the mouth. Later he can breathe in through the mouth, lower his face into the water, and breathe out forcibly blowing bubbles out from the mouth. A plastic bowl, filled with warm water,

20

can be put on the bathroom floor with a mirror on the bottom. The child can put his face right into the bowl to see himself and pull faces. This can be repeated in the large bath if a suitable plastic-framed mirror is used.

Do not try to hurry the progress when the time comes to take the child to the pool or the sea. When one hears of children swimming before they can walk it is usually in warmer climates than in Britain, with air and water temperatures which ensure a happy introduction to water play. The important thing is always to take time, and let the child build up confidence in his own way. He should be allowed to enjoy the sea and sand as he wishes. The sea is buoyant, but progress will only be made by daily dips, so do not try to teach him to swim in one easy lesson!

A 'Mother and Baby Class' is the ideal way to get toddlers used to a large expanse of water. In some towns these are already established but with considerable variations. There may be instruction for children of three to six years, accompanied in the water by an adult, who need not be a swimmer. There may be similar classes which cater for smaller children, from babes in arms to five years old. These classes may be linked with other recreational pursuits, such as a 'Keep Fit' class, for the mother whilst the toddler is entertained elsewhere. There are 'Water Babies Clubs' for children who have not started school; they must again be accompanied by an adult who need not be a swimmer. Instructions and arm bands are provided, and the aim of the club is, 'To make young children SAFE in or near the water and provide a basis for family recreation'.

My personal view is that a parent, preferably mother, should be in the water with the child, especially one under eighteen months. Occasionally a substitute might be needed, but even then the mother should be on the poolside always within sight of the child. Pregnant and nursing mothers can still swim, and there is no doubt that swimming can improve the figure, as the muscles supporting the breast are strengthened. Women wanting to 'get back into shape' will find that swimming will help them to do so. I think, too, that it is important that a mother should be a swimmer, and that the child sees her swimming before he ever accompanies her into the pool. Water confidence is catching, but so is water fear, so non-swimming mothers should set about learning for their families' sake, as well as their own.

If you join a 'Mother and Baby Class' or Club you will probably receive help and instruction from the person in charge, and this will vary according to the size of the class, the water depth, the ability range and the use made of inflated aids. Mostly the instruction will be of a relaxed and play-like nature, with no attempt at formal teaching and only of short duration. If such a class is non-existent in your area then try and organize a local group of like-minded women. See the pool authorities about booking it for your exclusive use, and try and get the assistance of an instructor. If this is not possible then someone must parade round the side as life-saver and 'look-out guard'. A person above water level can spot and prevent any likely unpleasant incident before it happens. Mothers wading backward can easily bump into each other, and be thrown off balance, which can frighten their children. If your child is frightened comfort him in the water, and do not get him out immediately. He should leave the pool with a pleasant memory of it, so any nervousness or fear must be dispelled quickly.

If you have a pool of your own then you have the advantage of being able to offer short daily lessons. It is the regularity of water experience which ensures progress just so long as it is pleasurable. The child must want to go in and not be forced in any way. Pool ownership can also represent a water hazard for small children in the neighbourhood, who do not know the word TRESPASS! Precautions in the shape of fencing should be taken.

If you are a good swimmer and prefer to 'go it alone' then take your child to the nearest heated pool regularly. A transfer from the bath at home to a pool should, if possible, mean a water temperature of at least 80° F., plus a warm-air temperature. Public pools of 72° F. or less lead to a rapid loss of body heat and resulting tension. If the pool is crowded you will do more harm than good, as the size, echoing noise and unfamiliar adult hurly burly will not make a visit to the pool the pleasure it should be. It is necessary to choose a time when the pool is practically empty and quiet. The child must be given time to adjust himself to his new surroundings and not be hustled into the water. At first he may prefer to sit on the side and watch you swim, but this will not be time wasted. You will be able to show how enjoyable it is in the water, and how it supports you and will support him. When he wants to join you, have your face level with his, and if he is very young then the head must be very carefully supported.

Gradually he will achieve breath control by always breathing through the mouth. This will be easier if he learns to float on the back first, water balance will also come with this, and very much later co-ordination to enable him to propel himself through the water. If he can walk when you first go to the pool then let him do this in the water, with shoulders under, and so get used to the water pressure against his body. This may cause him to hold his breath, so have a duck, so that he can push it along and say, 'Quack! Quack!', or blow a table tennis ball or balloon, as it is breathing out which is important. In shallow water remember to bend or kneel down to keep your face on a level with the child's. Some learner pools have steps leading down into them, and these are most useful for the child to sit on until ready to go into the pool. Later on he will want to jump off a step into your arms. You can show him how to put his hands on the steps, with arms straight, face out of the water and feet paddling behind. Later he can put his hands on the step behind him, lying on his back and kicking and splashing his feet in front. He will not concentrate for long, so frequent changes of activity will be necessary. Inflatable arm bands, a jacket, polystyrene floats which fit into pockets on the front or back of a costume or waistcoat, or a ring can be used. Arm bands have the advantage of allowing him to put his face in the water. If the child is very small a ring could be too big, unless it has a centre skirt, or tapes are fixed to it like braces. The Royal Society for the Prevention of Accidents quite rightly stresses that inflatable aids and supporting toys should only be used under strict supervision. Let him realize from the start that it is the water, plus the aid, which is holding him up. Even if you are only holding him lightly you must give him confidence, especially on his back, or he may twist round and overbalance and give himself a real fright. When he wants to start moving through the water he will do 'what comes naturally' and you can start from there. Little fat girls often float on their backs like corks, then windmill their arms and splash their feet in an embryonic back crawl. Other children windmill their arms on the front, but here the breathing is not so easy. Some kick out sideways like a frog, and as the face is clear and they see where they are going, they propel themselves forward with a variety of arm movements. You are not concerned with a proper stroke at this stage, as your aims are for the child to be able to float and propel himself towards safety.

When real progress is being made and he does not need you holding him, start letting a little air out of his inflated aid. This is very necessary with some children who become dependent on their rings and refuse to give them up. Never take off a single arm band as this will make him lop-sided. When the inflated aid is practically empty of air try holding one end of a polystyrene float whilst he holds the other. Walk backwards whilst he propels himself forward by kicking his legs. Alternatively he can hold the float on his chest and kick with his legs whilst you walk beside him. This float will not give him the same support as a body aid from which he is gradually being weaned. The moment will come, and this will be a very gradual thing, when he is propelling himself with no aid other than your assuring presence within easy reach. The next stage is learning a swimming stroke and you may find you are not the best person to help. Perhaps father, or a relative, friend or swimming coach, comes into the picture here, but many factors will need to be taken into account. If a basis of happiness and security in the water has been laid, then progress will continue. But the pace must be suitable for the individual child. For some the pace must not be forced, whereas with others it is necessary to present a constant challenge. A co-ordinated stroke is learnt by trial and error, by experimentation and discovery, by constant repetition and concentration. The same play-like lines should be used, and the adult must remember that the pupil is only a CHILD! (*See Plates 1(a) and (b), 260.*)

CHILDREN

Parents should be careful about letting non-swimming children go to the pool alone, or with a crowd of friends. What if he is ducked under, thrown in or dared to go out of his depth? It is essential, too, to check a child's report that he can swim. Children are very imaginative. I once motored an eight-year-old country boy to the town pool as he assured me that he could swim. When I got in and waited for him to join me he said, 'I didn't know you had to take your feet off the bottom.' This may seem extreme, but there are far too many children who are convinced that they are good swimmers when they are very inadequate. They manage well enough in the local pool, but no pool can reproduce the hazards of inland waters and the sea.

If you go to the pool with your child you will be able to judge whether he is safe to play unsupervised in water hazard areas. Boys will always be boys and no one wants to curb their spirit of adventure, which leads to the building of rafts, and Tarzan-like rope swinging across streams. All such inventive and imaginative play is great fun for the swimmer, but it is risky for the non-swimmer or 'struggler'. Weaker swimmers must be given instruction and encouragement. Take a real interest in your child's progress, and frame his first swimming certificate, as it will only too soon be replaced by posters or pinups. With children learning to swim at a much earlier age, and standards rising daily, there is no other sport in which such rapid progress can be made whilst still young. It is possible for a child to be a non-swimmer at the beginning of the season and a Gold Survival Award winner at the end. Award fees and payment for badges all mount up, but swimming is not an expensive sport, and money should not be begrudged if it means working hard to acquire personal survival and life-saving skills. Costumes tend to resemble 'Joseph's coat of many colours' with all the badges sewn on, but although the badge collecting stage will pass, the skills will remain.

TEENAGERS

A non-swimming teenager, especially a boy, can present a real problem. He may have lacked the opportunity to learn, or perhaps dodged swimming lessons, or failed to progress and given a distorted picture of his ability to his parents. One such boy built himself a canoe and was drowned. The parents thought he could swim. Youth Clubs, Guides, Scouts and other Association's swimming classes might be the solution, and this problem is being tackled at many new school and community pools. Teenage pupils, having contributed money or labour without the benefit of swimming in the pool, have *teen* classes organized for them. Private lessons from the local coach, or sessions at the pool when friends are not there to laugh, might also help.

A boy enjoys teaching his girl friend to swim, and teenage girls are usually less diffident about learning to swim. They appreciate that swimming is not a sport that will make them muscular, and that they will look attractive in a bathing costume in their teens.

COACHES

Most coaches are now well qualified, and have taken the examination of the Amateur Swimming Association, Swimming Teachers' Association and Royal Life Saving Society. If there is not a local coach you could inquire of these associations for guidance. Some coaches specialize, but the majority cover as many aspects as their pool conditions, and their time in it, allow. As I have already said, coaches at seaside resorts and residential courses often achieve excellent results, because they give their pupils a daily lesson, which is the ideal. The pupil also has the time to practise and consolidate new skills, between these lessons. Try to avoid a weekly lesson in favour of three times a week, at least in the early learning stages. Coaches' methods are purely individual, and vary considerably, and they have their own ideas, too, as to whether one stroke should be taught first, or there should be multiple stroke tuition. Naturally most coaches will fit their training to suit the individual pupil, whether an adult, teenager or child. With a fairly young child some coaches like the parents to be present, and others ask them to leave. The latter is no reflection on the parent, but the coach's policy is often influenced by the pool facilities. If you wish to be with your child you should check up on this point. The end result for all pupils should combine good technique, with sufficient stamina to want to continue to progress in pleasurable watermanship.

Good swimming clubs usually employ their own coach, and membership of such a club can lead to social as well as recreative benefits. Big clubs, with more time in a pool, organize a novice to expert programme, which may include competitive swimming, diving, water polo, survival swimming, life saving, water ballet and synchronized swimming. Coaches take their promising club members to competitive events, various training clinics and residential courses. Today there are competitions for all stages; from school, county, Age Group, English Schools' Swimming Association, Amateur Swimming Association, Commonwealth and Olympic Games. Boys, but more especially girls, can become champions whilst still at school. Sometimes a situation develops where the parents, coach, club and school are pulling against each other, and the child's loyalties are divided. As the good of the child is the only consideration, everyone concerned should constantly check their motives.

TEACHERS

Compulsory school games are now less prevalent, but swimming should be compulsory, because of its life-saving potential. This is not yet possible because of the lamentable lack of water space, which, in some densely populated areas, may mean only one season's tuition in swimming, as late or later, than the age of eleven years! In some rural areas it can mean no swimming tuition. However, teachers have shown a lead here, and with the co-operation of parents, or the whole local community, hundreds of pools have been built.

A school swimming class can consists of as many as thirty children; and can range from a 100 per cent non-swimming group, to a group of a very wide ability range. Incredible as it may seem, there are still children whose first experience of being completely surrounded by water is at their first swimming lesson. However, teachers can, and do, cope, and in spite of the class numbers get the great majority of their pupils swimming. Teaching methods vary according to conditions. Some schools having shallow learner pools adopt the shallow water method. Some teachers favour the single stroke method initially, usually either breast-stroke or front crawl. Others prefer the multiple stroke method in which children swim on the front and the back. More use is made of aids to get the pupils moving and away from the poolside. However, whatever method is used, a class of non-swimmers will not make uniform progress, but will gradually sort itself out into ability groups. The more proficient ones will be given purposeful activities to follow from a blackboard, or instruction cards in pencil on the poolside. The more competent children can draw up their own training schedules, in consultation with the teacher, and use the deeper water. In this way the teacher has a check on whether or not the programmes are being followed. Sometimes ropes are used across and down the pool to pen pupils into different ability groups. To progress from the sheeps' to the goats' pen is an incentive in itself.

When there are two teachers, or a teacher and the official pool coach, it is much easier, as the class can be divided into ability groups and more rapid progress made. With two it is possible for one of them to enter the water occasionally, to help the very nervous children. The other teacher then has to keep a careful watch over all. A single teacher in charge of a class cannot go into the water, except at the very end of the lesson when the majority of pupils are getting dressed.

Most Local Education Authorities either give graded certificates themselves, or arrange for the various national awards to be taken. This should mean that no pupil is swiming about aimlessly. The first certificate is the most important and the school teacher's main task is to teach the pupils to swim. The Dolphin Trophy Scheme has acted as a big incentive for primary schools aiming to have every leaver able to swim. Details of the scheme can be obtained from the English Schools' Swimming Association.

In rural areas the stumbling block to progress is usually the lack of practice between weekly lessons. Where schools are able to block their pool time and have a daily visit to the pool for three or four consecutive weeks, quicker and better results are achieved. Schools with their own pools leap ahead, especially if the pool is covered. Good swimming schools keep record cards of progress, have a well-stocked library of swimming and allied sports books, and all the necessary impedimenta such as swimming aids, stopwatches, rubber bricks, 'Kiss of Life' models, etc.

NATIONAL TECHNICAL OFFICERS

The Department of Education and Science gives grant aid for the employment of National Technical Officers to assist with the development of life saving. Their work covers experiments in new techniques, liaison with Branches, Honorary Representatives, Life Guard Corps Clubs and organization of conventions on instruction and examination. Details from the Royal Life Saving Society.

The Amateur Swimming Association's technical officers

give theoretical and practical help to District Associations, clubs, colleges, school teachers, 'Learn to Swim' campaigns, élite swimmers and the organization of courses. Details from the Amateur Swimming Association and the Central Council of Physical Recreation.

POOL SUPERINTENDENTS

Pool Superintendents, or Bath Managers, are usually members of The Institute of Bath Management and can give help on queries relating to pool maintenance. Their co-operation should always be sought if the best use is to be made of the facilities under their jurisdiction.

Reference Books

Your Book of Swimming, Margaret Jarvis (Faber and Faber Limited)
Swimming (Know the Game)
Swimming and Diving, E.S.S.A. (William Heineman)
'Learning to Swim' (Swimming aids tested), *Which*, August 1967

3 · Water Wisdom

This chapter may well read as if I think there is no fun to be had swimming anywhere at anytime! However, if I save only one life by pointing out dangers, and alerting people, it will have been worth writing.

STATISTICS

In an article written in 1897 drownings in Great Britain were estimated at 6,000 to 7,000 a year. In spite of the increase, and greater mobility, of today's population the figure has been brought down to about 1,000 a year. This figure is still not one for congratulation, as it represents heartache for many thousands, and recrimination for all of us when we know that half of our population cannot swim. The main causes are obvious—shortage and consequent overcrowding of pools, and lack of swimming lessons.

Inland waters account for about 75 per cent and the sea for about 25 per cent of the drowning accidents:

1961	1963	1965	1967	1969
per cent	per cent	per cent	per cent	per cent
76·5/23·5	76·2/23·8	73·15/26·85	76·74/23·26	72·58/27·42

Breakdown of Drowning Statistics

	1961	1963	1965	1967	1969
Accidents in homes	54	30	43	38	69
Bathing and paddling	165	167	101	156	177
*Children playing near water	172	129	144	159	119

	1961	1963	1965	1967	1969
Elderly people	23	16	20	62	16
Home-made rafts	13	12	11	10	7
Fall from cliffs	6	5	5	7	2
Cut off by tide	10	0	10	7	10
Diving, Sub-Aqua	7	4	4	5	10
Fishing	34	17	26	22	25
Boats	161	119	144	132	157
Vehicles	26	37	28	26	21
Influence of drink	33	32	44	32	51
Ice	1	†27	11	6	13

* Majority under 5 years of age   † Hard winter

SAFETY RULES

These will vary from family to family, but safe swimming means being water fit. This entails not bathing with open wounds, foot or skin infections, ear trouble or catarrh, when recovering from illness or when feeling unwell. It also means not swimming when hungry or exhausted, overheated or for at least an hour after a meal. This last advice is often ignored, but my father brought from the bottom of a crowded pool, but failed to revive, a champion swimmer. The man had gone to the pool after a heavy meal, dived in unnoticed, and failed to surface again. He was only missed when he was needed to swim in a team race. It is also a mistake to stay in so long that one is thoroughly chilled, and one's efficiency reduced. A swim is best followed by a cold, not hot, shower, and a brisk rub-down with a roughish towel. Time to dry properly is important, especially between the toes, as it is easy to get dead white skin there otherwise. With young children, and people with sensitive skins, care should be taken not to get sunburnt.

C   33

Learn to swim when young, and supervise children playing near water. Never swim alone, dive or jump into unknown waters, or where there is not sufficient depth. Never indulge in horseplay, scare, duck, or throw into the water people who are nervous or non-swimmers—this can put them off swimming for life. Never pretend to be in difficulties as this could endanger someone else's life. In inland waters and the sea, remain waist deep, and in the sea swim parallel with the shore. Inflated toys should not be used in open waters unless tied to a rope, or adequately supervised. A swimmer should never attempt to rescue balls or airbeds in the sea. However, if you are caught by an outgoing tide, then hang on to the inflated article as this will give support, and be more easily spotted by rescuers. Always take home or dispose of litter in receptacles, especially bottles and tins.

Adequate supervision can only be given by a swimmer, capable of taking the necessary safety precautions, and of showing good judgement. For a person in charge of a group in a pool, a whistle is useful to curb unruliness and screaming. Any rescue equipment, such as a reaching pole or lifebuoy should be within reach. It might be safer in some instances to divide the deep from the shallow end by a rope. It is much easier to be in control of a group if you are dressed appropriately and able to jump in without ruining good clothes. If you are in the water, then the best position is one in which the majority of the group are in front of you. If the group is a large one, then someone else should be on the poolside helping to supervise when you are in the water.

A supervisor must be able to judge when swimmers are ready to move into deeper water, or to attempt a dive. Swimmers can both over-estimate and under-estimate their capabilities, and here the timely warning or necessary spur will be needed. Swimming in cold open waters means extra care, and only a small number should be supervised by one person.

SAFETY TRAINING

Ideally, everyone should be able to swim well enough to survive in an emergency. The Amateur Swimming Association have Bronze, Silver and Gold Personal Survival Awards. The Royal Life Saving Society have a Water Safety Award for inexperienced and non-swimmers, and Preliminary and Advanced Safety Awards. Their graded awards in life saving techniques ensure that competent swimmers are in control of an emergency, so that they will not risk their own life in a hopeless situation, but can give aid to someone in difficulty or danger in the water. Too often would-be rescuers drown because they have not sized up the situation correctly, and have not acted within the limits of their ability. The Royal Life Saving Society recommend the following order:

REACH; THROW; WADE; ROW; SWIM;   TOW
                                 (taking a   (if trained
                                 support)   life saver)

A towing rescue should never be attempted if the swimmer, after an outward swim, lacks the stamina necessary for possible defensive methods, or release skills, to gain control of a frantic victim, plus a safe tow and landing.

Drownproofing
This is a survival technique which enables a swimmer to stay afloat for hours on end, even under the most adverse conditions. It was devised by the late Fred Lanoue, swimming coach at the Georgia Institute of Technology, U.S.A. Coaching in this method could be sought, failing which his explanatory book should be read.

35

Survival floating

Family fun can result from trying out different survival floats.

EXAMPLES

Float in lifebuoy or life-jacket making sure that you are able to remain face upward. Float holding on to a canoe paddle, oar, water skis or upturned dinghy. Float holding on to a plank of wood, rubber ball, upturned plastic bucket, or on to Wellington boots under each arm. Float wearing inflated clothing round neck, under stomach like water wings, or between ankles. In fact use any possible flotsam and jetsam material to practise survival floating.

However, nothing can really take the place of progressive safety training in survival, or life-saving classes to achieve the necessary skills.

Kiss of life

Newspapers have made almost everyone familiar with the value of this method of resuscitation, and its wide application.

'Mum's kiss saves baby.' The baby, aged two, was found floating face downward in a slime-covered pit.

'Neighbour gives kiss of life.' A mother rushed into the next-door house with her child whose head was in a plastic bag. The neighbour revived the child.

'Two save one.' A strong swimmer rescued a man who was not breathing when landed. A non-swimmer revived the man with the kiss of life, which the rescuer did not know how to give.

Everyone ought to learn how to give this method of resuscitation. When breathing has stopped, as a result of poisonous gas, car exhaust and smoke; electric and lightning shock; suffocation; throat blockage and strangulation as well as drowning, immediate action must be taken by whoever is on the spot. There is no excuse for ignorance. The method must be learnt at first hand from experts.

A simple home-made model can then be used for practice. Surgeon-Captain Stanley Miles has devised such a model and described it in *Family Doctor* and on 'Panorama'. It consists of a $\frac{1}{2}$-gallon sealed tin the size of a head, into which a mouth $1\frac{1}{2}$ in. by $\frac{1}{4}$ in. is made, the sharp edges folded inward. The nose is made by inserting tightly an inch of rubber tubing and cutting it obliquely. On the opposite side of the tin 18 in. of $\frac{1}{4}$-in. rubber tubing is inserted. An 8-in. square plastic bag is then secured to the tubing with an elastic band. A heavy book allowing a rhythm of 10 to 12 cycles a minute is placed on the plastic bag. To represent a child casualty the bag is folded in half and a smaller book used. Both the mouth-to-mouth and mouth-to-nose techniques can be practised in this way. (*See Plate 3a.*)

RESCUE AIDS

Pools

Far too many pools have rescue equipment which is too heavy or is out of sight. Many are short of items of First Aid materials, including resuscitation equipment. The telephone numbers of hospital and nearby doctors should be prominently displayed, and the telephone should not be in a room which is locked at night when clubs are using the pool. There is a pool alarm on the market which sounds if anyone accidentally falls into an unattended pool.

Pools in holiday resorts and at hotels are often large, or oddly shaped, and sometimes insufficient control is exercised. This can lead to small children being lost to view, non-swimmers going into deep water wearing inflated aids, or floating there on airbeds. It sometimes happens that in-experienced divers are 'thrown over' by springboards, either because they have not taken time, or because they have not been allowed time, to get the 'feel' of the board. In a crowded and unfamiliar pool it is very easy for accidents to happen unnoticed—a diver may not surface again; a boy may float unconscious face down, wearing a mask; no-one may spot another boy diving off boards diagonally so as to surface at the poolside, because he can dive, but not swim! The essential need in such pools is an attendant patrolling, or seated like a tennis umpire with an overall view of the pool.

Domestic pools could have a stout post to which is attached an upright bamboo reaching pole, or a lifebuoy, inner tube, or Dunlop quoit and line, hanging on a hook for throwing. Also on the post could be a cellophane-covered telephone number of the hospital or doctor, and a 4 in. × 3 in. Kiss of Life illustration. (Ernest Benn Ltd., Bouverie House, Fleet Street, London, E.C.4.)

Beaches

Beaches can be steep shelving, rocky, with small inlets or sandbanks easily cut off by the tide, large seaweed beds, jellyfish, strong undertow or surf, or deposits of oil.

If you have small children choose a resort with a safe, clean beach, preferably patrolled by life guards. Adults should heed local rules and advice. Weak or non-swimmers, often jacket-less jackasses too, who hire water craft, can endanger the lives of others who may have to go to their rescue. Water skiers, or outboard motorists, who do not obey their limitation rules, can present another hazard.

Abroad many English people prefer isolation, and dive off rocks for an enjoyable swim well away from everyone else. However, getting out can mean scratches, bruises and feet full of sea urchin needles. It then becomes obvious why the locals all wear fins or bathing shoes and enter and leave the water at one particular spot. The safest spot is usually where the local children are being taught to swim. Occasionally sub-aqua equipment can be hired abroad by those who have not had sufficient preliminary training. Adequate training and approved equipment is essential to be really safe.

Inland waters

Inland waters can be dangerous if they have steep sloping slippery banks. People dive in if the water is clear and then exhaust themselves trying to get out, especially if there are currents or the water is very cold. When the water is murky it is foolhardy to jump or dive in, as these waters often have unseen hazards, and are the dumping grounds for rubbish. Many neck and back injuries have resulted from diving into unknown waters. Known clean waters are delightful to swim in, but muddy bottoms, treacherous weeds, or fast-flowing rivers with weirs, are to be treated with respect, or avoided. Some rivers abroad are so lethal that one is advised not to dangle even a hand in them; the local population have either acquired immunity or died!

Touring holidays can mean a different and pleasant water experience every day, or the reverse, if care is not taken. To allow children to go for a swim whilst the tent is erected or caravan parked, has proved fatal on several occasions. It is a question of settling in first and spying out the land. Statistics show that it is the first and last holiday swim which are the most dangerous. The former because people are so anxious to have a 'quick dip' that they take risks, though unwittingly. The latter because they are over confident, and hurry to get a last swim before returning home; for some it is really the last swim.

Life guards

The Corps of Canoe Life Guards and Life Guard Corps are composed of volunteers who patrol popular bathing places inland and at the sea. In Cornwall twenty-two people were drowned one year, but this was reduced to eight in the following two years, when fifty people were saved by surf life-savers and fourteen by the police. No drownings occurred where there were beach patrols. In Hastings there is a bye-law enabling the corporation to prosecute those who disregard warning notices. The beach is divided into seven sections where bathing may be prohibited when flags are flying. Life guards in boats are strategically placed, but four children were drowned a cliff's walk away from Hastings, on an isolated beach without a patrol. The Royal Society for the Prevention of Accidents' flag safety code is now widely adopted:

A red flag = danger, no patrol.

Two half-red, half-yellow flags = life guard patrols between them.

A squared black and white flag = surfboard riding area only.

Obviously the great majority of open waters cannot be adequately supervised, but more equipment could be strategically placed by local authorities. Unfortunately vandals often damage such equipment and replacement becomes costly. Another problem is that women and children find an ordinary lifebuoy too heavy to throw accurately. Dunlop's have developed a small lightweight rubber quoit attached to a long nylon lifeline, to meet this need. Also there is now a 25-oz. buoy which can be thrown, pushed or towed, and supports at least two people.

However, the greatest need is for a National Life Guard Service which could co-ordinate all the emergency aids such as helicopters, life boats and specially designed rescue boats.

They would need to be equipped with walkie talkie apparatus, telephones, reel and line, lookout posts, resuscitation and First Aid equipment, headquarters and transport.

Reference books:
Handbook, Royal Life Saving Society
Your Book of Survival Swimming and Life Saving, Margaret Jarvis (Faber and Faber Limited)
Drownproofing, Fred Lanoue (Herbert Jenkins)
Water Safety Code, Code for Juniors, Charts, Leaflets, Quiz = *How safe are our beaches—as safe as the people who play on them.* (It illustrates typical hazards which can cause drowning fatalities.)
Guide for Local Authorities: all from the Royal Society for the Prevention of Accidents
'Lifejackets and Buoyancy Aids', *Which*, June 1970

4 · Watermanship

For continued progress in swimming, new challenges and goals must be constantly found. Many of these are provided by working for national certificates and awards, but even in training for these a swimmer may become stale through lack of variety. The non-competitive skills in this chapter should help to bring enjoyment to every visit to the pool. Many of them can be practised alone or with a friend. They may also be useful for club, school and group sessions, when a wider selection of skills can be made.

CROSSING THE POOL SKILLS

Solo

Front glide

Put one foot on the pool side, lean forward, breathe in and put face in water between arms as hands push forward together. Give a strong push with feet and keep head well down so that heels come to surface.

Back glide

Tuck toes under rail, lean backward and glide. Complete width by sculling with hands at sides. Alternatively, throw arms strongly overhead into glide position and complete width by back paddling with legs.

Bicycling

Tread water, using breast stroke arms, and legs as if riding a bicycle to cross pool in a vertical position.

Broken arm
Swim on back or side using only one arm.

Broken leg
Swim using arms only and one leg, and let the 'broken' leg drift.

Broken arm and leg
Swim using one arm and one leg on opposite sides of the body. Reverse.

Breast stroke underwater
Surface when breath gives out, even if width is not crossed.

Twin tail
A combination of front, back and side paddle. Start with dog paddle, or paddle with hands at sides; turn over on to left side for side paddle, on to back for back paddle and on to right side, continuously.

Waltzing Mathilda
A combination of front and back crawl; left arm pulls for front crawl, turn over on to back and right arm pulls for back crawl, continuously. Reverse.

Front glide underwater
As for front glide, but push hands down towards pool bottom. To surface again turn finger tips upward.

Back glide underwater
As for back glide, but keep head well back.

Porpoise
Scull face downward; drop head and swing legs up vertically

43

for a surface dive. Continue to scull underwater then raise head, hollow back, regain surface and take breath. Repeat.

Sculling head first

On back with ears at water level, body perfectly straight, toes pointed, shoulders and elbows relaxed and hands by sides. With bent wrists and finger-tips pointing to the surface push both hands simultaneously outwards and then pull them inwards to scull, head leading.

Sculling feet first

Reverse the action of head first sculling by bending wrists so that finger-tips point to pool bottom to scull, feet leading.

Propeller

On back with arms extended beyond head. Bend wrists, palms facing away from head, and scull with feet leading.

Torpedo

Similar to *propeller*, but the body sinks beneath the surface with only the heels above water, and travels with feet leading. At first this is achieved by a slight bend at the waist and sculling from the wrists with an upward pressure. Later on the body should be kept in a straight line.

Side sculling

On back, then turn on left side with right arm over head and scull with left hand under body, head leading. Repeat on right side.

Switchback propeller

On back as for *propeller*, then scull down to pool bottom and to surface lift feet and scull upward. Repeat.

Submarine
On back, raise one leg vertically keeping other leg and body horizontal. Scull on surface head leading, then sink underwater (periscope) with quick sculling action and surface again. Take breath and repeat.

Walking on the water
On back with arms at sides or crossed on chest. Bend right knee vigorously drawing the right instep under body. Simultaneously stretch the left leg gently forward upward relaxing instep. Alternate leg action clockwise, keeping knees under water.

Houdini
Hands tied together loosely, back paddle either scooping with hands on alternate sides, or holding them extended beyond head. With feet tied, instead of hands, swim breast, front crawl, or back crawl arm stroke.

Swimming backward feet leading
On front, facing poolside, extend arms in line with body, scull with hands shoulder width apart with leg paddle under water, feet leading.

Canoe
On front with head and heels raised and body arched. Hands by sides, finger-tips pointing to pool bottom, palms facing feet, scull towards and away from mid line of body, head leading.

Fish
Push off from side to pool bottom and scull as for 'Canoe'.

Seal

In 'Canoe' position lower head, raise legs and scull beneath the water. Hold head well back and scull to regain surface. Take breath and repeat.

Duck

On front with head high and hands sculling under body. Bend knees up to a right angle, cross ankles to make a 'tail'. If performing this skill for a display add a few 'Quack! Quacks!'

Crab

Face end of pool on front with the arms bent, elbows outward, and the hands sculling alternately sideways under the face. The knees are bent like a frog's and alternately bend and stretch sideways to progress crablike across the pool.

Loop the loop

Dive to pool bottom, push off to surface, somersault backward to pool bottom, push off to surface at poolside. Alternatively dive to bottom, float to surface, somersault backward and float to side.

Fig. 1. Loop the Loop

Pairs

Leapfrog
In shallow water either the leaper puts hands on partner's back for a jump, or dives over back without touching.

Tandem breast stroke
Breast stroke joined with number 2 holding on to number 1's waist.

Tandem back stroke
Back stroke with number 1 holding on to number 2's shoulders.

Tandem front crawl
Front crawl with number 1's legs round number 2's waist or neck.

Tandem back crawl
Back crawl with number 1's legs round number 2's waist or neck.

Tug and liner
Number 2 swims breast stroke with number 1's feet gripping either side of neck. Number 1 floats on back sculling with hands or arms folded.

Barges
Number 2 swims breast stroke leg kick grasping number 1's ankles. Number 1 floats on back sculling with hands, head leading.

Canoeing
Neck linkage, number 1 back crawls and number 2 front crawls with arms matching.

Rowing

Neck linkage, number 1 uses arms as in English back stroke and number 2 swims butterfly breast stroke, keeping in time with each other.

Tired swimmer

Number 1 on back, legs together or parted, and elbows straight, holds number 2's shoulders. Number 2 swims breast stroke.

Pair sculling

(a) Partners float on back facing same way with number 2's feet gripping number 1's neck. Either both scull with hands at sides, feet leading, or number 2 can scull in the 'Propeller' position.

(b) Repeat neck linkage in reverse, either both scull, head leading, or number 2 also assists with foot paddling.

(c) Number 1's feet under number 2's armpits. Either both scull, head leading, or number 2 assists with foot paddling.

(d) Repeat armpit linkage, both scull, feet leading.

(e) Inside hand on partner's shoulder, with elbows straight, outside hand sculling, head leading. Repeat with arms round waists.

(f) Neck linkage, pair prone float and *canoe* scull, head leading.

(g) Neck linkage, number 1 floats on back and sculls, head leading. Number 2 prone floats and *canoe* sculls, head leading.

(h) Ankle linkage, number 1 sculls for head leading, and number 2 for feet leading.

Waltzing

Side by side, partners start with inside arms front crawl,

1a. Mother and baby enjoying their pool visit (*see p. 25*)

1b. Nine-month-old boy floating (*see p. 25*)

2a. Water Babies Club watch a 4-year-old mile
swimmer (*see p. 25*)

2b. Deaf-blind boys enjoying a 'Push Off' contest
(*see pp. 15 and 85*)

3a. 'Kiss of Life' practice with home-made model
(*see p. 37*)

3b. 'Kiss of Life' given when able to stand in water
(*see p. 36*)

4a. 'Frogmen's Frolic'. Frogmen about to enter pool
(*see p. 90*)

4b. 'Frogmen's Frolic'. Frogmen do handstands
on pool bottom (*see p. 90*)

5a. Moses' mother and sister hide him in the bulrushes (*see p. 88*)

5b. Pharaoh's daughter leaves with Moses (*see p. 88*)

6a. Sub-Aqua groups under instruction (*see p. 91*)

6b. Underwater Hockey. York Sub-Aqua Club (*see p. 91*)

7. Home-built raft race on River Severn (*see p.* 87)

8a. Wheelbarrow race on supported planks (*see p. 81*)

8b. Viking Raid Race (*see p. 83*)

then outside arms, then inside arms, turn over away from each other and back crawl with inside, outside and inside arms. Repeat turning towards each other.

Three legged
Side by side, with inside ankles loosely tied to partner's, for either front or back crawl joined.

Siamese twins
Side by side with inside wrists loosely tied to partner's for either front or back crawl joined. Very good swimmers can tie both ankles and wrists, but should only attempt this in shallow water as perfect timing is essential.

Mirror
Partners face each other and push off from poolside. Number 1 swims breast stroke on surface, and number 2 underwater 'mirrors' 1's stroke on the back.

Shadow
Repeat 'Mirror', but both swim breast stroke with number 1 keeping time with number 2.

Threes
Select from solo crossings and add formations:

Triangle formation
Number 2 leads, with numbers 1 and 3 in line, either all crossing in the same way, or number 1 different.

Line formation
Take cue from the left and keep in a straight line.

File formation
Keep the two spaces equal.

D   49

Cannon formation
Lead from left to right with two spaces equal.

Trio sculling
Side by side with hands on shoulders, numbers 1 and 3 scull
with outside hand, head first leading, and all three back
paddle.

Odd man out
Number 2 back paddles with hands on inside shoulder of
1 and 3, who both dog paddle forward.

Fours
Select from solo and pair crossings and add formations:

Line, file and cannon formations

Odds and evens formation
Numbers 1 and 3 start, followed by 2 and 4, and keep both
lines straight.

Square formation
Numbers 1 and 2 in front, with 3 and 4 behind, making an
evenly spaced square.

Diamond formation
Number 1 in front, 2 and 3 behind, and 4 behind 1, making
an evenly spaced diamond.

Fives
Line, file, cannon, odds and evens formations

Flight formation
Number 3 leads, then 2 and 4, followed by 1 and 5, making
an evenly spaced flight formation.

Domino formation
Numbers 1 and 2, 4 and 5 in two lines, with 3 in the middle to make a Domino 5.

Maltese cross formation
Numbers 1, 3 and 5 in a file, with 2, 3 and 4 in line, all evenly spaced.

Large Groups
There are endless possible permutations:
  Triangle, Flight, Triangle.
  Lines crossing in waves sculling.
  Odds and evens tandem breast stroke.

MIDDLE OF THE POOL SKILLS

Solo
Backward somersault
On back with arms at sides, palms downward. Draw knees up to chest, press head backward, lift feet and push water downward. Take breath and repeat.

Forward somersault
Tread water with arms sideways, draw knees up to chest, drop head forward and scoop arms downwards, forwards and upwards. Take breath and repeat.

Spinning top
Float vertically with arms folded on surface. Push with one foot whilst other foot pulls so as to spin in direction of pulling foot.

Washing tub
On back, draw parted knees up to chest with ankles crossed.

Scull with one hand towards body and the other away so as to rotate.

Water wheel
On right side with left hand on hip. The right hand can either be used to help scull round, or be placed under head. The legs alternatively cycle forward clockwise.

Full length backward somersault
Float on back, then press the head backward hollowing back, and sweep arms forward and downward. Keep legs together with knees slightly bent and straighten out horizontally on surface. Take breath and repeat.

Full length forward somersault
Float face downward, and surface dive into vertical position. Then bend head forward and press water downward so as to surface again. Take breath and repeat.

Monkey up the stick
Stand in shallow water, and make a high jump out of water with arms shooting upward overhead. Then drop down under water and stand on hands shooting legs upward. Repeat.

Circle propeller
Propel with right hand only, left hand on head, counterclockwise. Repeat clockwise with change of hands.

Figure 8 propeller
Propel with one hand only, other on head, then reverse hands when necessary to make a figure 8.

Corkscrew
Sink to bottom of pool, and use speed to 'water wheel' clockwise upward to surface.

Stationary sculling

On back arms close to body, hands at surface fingers level with wrists. Scull with palms facing pool bottom, and adjust speed of sculling action so as to remain stationary.

Dipping and rising

Tread water at deep end, then raise arms sideways upwards until they meet above out of water. Sink down, and when hands are below surface propel with them upwards, causing body to sink to bottom of pool. Push off with feet, and drive arms sideways, downwards in order to surface again. Repeat.

Pairs

Meeting and parting

Numbers 1 and 2 surface dive from opposite sides, to meet with finger-tips at bottom and middle of pool, and so rise to surface, then scull backward away from each other to starting place.

Over and under

Float facing same way, with number 1 holding on to number 2's ankles. Number 1 then pulls underneath causing number 2 to pass over the top. Eyes must be kept open so that number 1 can time her surfacing, so that her feet float into position for number 2 to grasp. Repeat the exchange.

Double somersault

Float facing same way, with number 1's feet round number 2's neck. So joined, both perform full length backward somersaults, with number 2's feet dropping backward for number 1 to grasp and put round her neck. Subsequent

53

joined somersaults are possible, if a breath is taken each time on surfacing.

Broomstick surface dive
Number 1 holds shortened broomstick, and swims towards centre and surface dives with it. Number 2 glides down from opposite side, so that in the middle she is able to glide between partner's arms and over stick, both finishing on opposite sides of pool.

Bouncing ball
Partners stand facing each other in chest-high water. Number 1 places both hands on number 2's head, for gentle push right under the water. Number 2 then springs up high from pool bottom with body upright, hands at sides. Repeat.

Buoyancy test
Number 1 floats on back, and number 2 puts hands on partner's chest to push number 1 gently under water. When number 1 floats to the surface again, repeat.

Shoulder waterwheel
Facing away from each other, clasp partner's hands with elbows straight and arms at right angles sideways. With head resting on partner's shoulder, waterwheel clockwise.

Hand waterwheel
Repeat, but grasp partner's right hand with elbow straight beyond head, and waterwheel clockwise.

Head to tail
Facing towards each other side by side on backs, grasp partner's shin, and scull head first backward in circle. Repeat with outside knee bent.

Scissors
Repeat with number 1 floating on top of number 2, grasping each other's ankles. Number 1 opens and closes 2's legs. Number 2 repeats. Both open and close legs together.

Threes
Triple somersault
As for *double somersault*, but number 3 drops feet backward for number 1 to grasp and put round her neck.

Hoop la
Tie three hoops above each other to brick, and surface dive and swim through them together.

Large Groups
Pulling support
Hold hands in large circle, even numbers walk forward into centre, bending arms to pull odd numbers inward, who perform either breast stroke or front crawl leg kick. Repeat outward, with even numbers walking backward pulling odd numbers lying on backs, for either back stroke or back crawl leg kick.

Circle support
Even numbers make circle holding hands, and odd numbers undergrasp two wrists, as on back with feet out of the circle, either for back stroke or back crawl leg kick. Repeat with holders walking slowly clockwise.

Wheel
Large circle evenly spaced, perform solo breast stroke, front crawl, sculling feet first, or pair sculling, tandem etc.

Wheels within wheels
Large circle breaks up into small circles, and back to large circle again.

FLOATING

Whether one can float easily or not depends upon the density of one's body, and the density of the media in which one is immersed. Some large-boned people, or those with hard muscles or too little flesh, find floating very difficult. However, the density of the human body changes with one's age, and someone who has never floated may find that they are successful later on in life. We all know that it is easier to float in the sea than in a pool, because the salt makes the water denser. I once floated half out of the Dead Sea as it was quite impossible to swim! So try floating in the sea, if you fail in the pool, and make yourself aware of the necessary adjustments of breathing and balance. Natural floaters should try these skills:

Skills for Solo Floaters
Revolving
Practice revolving over, from the supine to prone floating position continuously until breath gives out, then float on back.

Round the Clock
Repeat 'Revolving', except that sufficient muscular action is made in the left side of the body for feet to remain in centre, whilst body makes a circle clockwise.

Pendulum
Float on back, and slowly bring arms from behind head
56

sideways, forwards on the surface. Simultaneously bend hips and lower legs downwards, upwards, backwards to finish in prone floating position. Reverse, by raising head and carrying arms sideways backward to beyond head.

Oyster
Float on back with arms beyond head. Jack-knife hips for fingers to touch toes, and hold position until back is on surface, with fingers and toes pointing to pool bottom. Straighten out slowly into the prone floating position. Repeat by rolling over from prone to supine float position.

Turtle's sunbath
Prone float, with head well down and hands just out of the water, legs parted and knees bent so that only the soles of the feet are also out of the water. Flap hands and feet lazily, but in variable order, as if they are flippers.

Supported floating for large group
When there are a sufficient number of like minded people, a few simple supported floating figures can be attempted. If necessary the less buoyant floaters can wear aids in the early stages, such as rubber rings or arm bands; hold polystyrene float behind head or between feet; small polystyrene float behind head or between feet; small polystyrene float inside costume at back of waist, or attached to belt.

Fan
Float close together, hand clasp with elbows bent and feet held by one or two supports, who are standing. Floaters stretch elbows to open fan out whilst supports remain stationary.

Wheel
Three or more supports stand back to back, holding feet of nine or more, hand clasp floaters. Alternatively the floaters' feet can be supported on an inner tube or lifebuoy.

Clock
As for 'Wheel', but with twelve floaters and four supports.

Catherine wheel
A support stands aside a hoop holding it. Floaters' hands grasp the hoop, whilst supports hold floaters' feet and walk the wheel slowly clockwise.

Supine circle
Odd numbers make a large circle, hands clasped floating on backs with feet in middle. Even numbers stand supporting odd numbers' feet. See progressions.

Prone circle
Repeat with odd numbers floating face down, feet outside circle for even numbers to support. See progressions.

Square
Numbers 1–4 stand at the four corners, giving hand clasp support to 5–8, who float on backs with feet in the middle. See progressions.

St. John's Cross
A support stands inside a hoop holding it. Inner floaters 2–5 grasp hoop with one foot on top and other underneath. Supports 6–9 hold 2–5 under shoulders. Supports stand or kneel according to water depth. Outer floaters 10–13 place feet on shoulder of supports 6–9. The cross is composed of eight floaters and five supports.

Water-lily

1–4 float with hands to centre, and 5–8 with feet. The 9–12 centre supports stand or kneel, each holding one floater's feet together with right hand, and next floater's hands together with left hand. The 13–20 outside supports hold the foot of one, and the hand of the next floater. The floaters with hands to centre part legs, and floaters with feet to centre have arms in star position. Eight floaters and eight or twelve supports are needed, but good floaters can substitute 9–12 centre supports for a lifebuoy.

PROGRESSIONS

Legs together, or parted, or one knee bent with only one foot supported. Supports can move the figure by swimming or walking. If latter is in shallow water the supports must bend knees so that their shoulders are under water. Supported floating is easier in a learner pool with the same depth overall, or a pool with a large shallow end.

5 · Water Games

These games are designed for a wide age and ability range with the exclusive use of a pool. At least one life-saving adult should be in charge and select those games most suitable for all those taking part. The number of swimmers must not be so large that too many are kept too long on the poolside waiting to play. The size of the pool and the apparatus which can safely be used in it will also determine choice. Although young children like to repeat their favourite games, older swimmers become bored if a game is played for too long or too often. The adult should give verdicts when applicable and select swimmers impartially.

CHANTING GAMES
(Adapted from Traditional Games and Rhymes)

Shallow water

Ring a' Roses

'Ring a' ring a' roses,
A pocket full of posies.
A Tishoo! A Tishoo!
All fall down.'

Walk round in small circles chanting rhyme, and on 'all fall down' drop down under water.

Pop, goes the Weasel

'Half a pound of twopenny rice,
Half a pound of treacle;
That's the way the money goes,
Pop, goes the weasel.'

Walk round in small circles with a 'weasel' in the centre. On 'Pop' he jumps up high and drops down under water. Change 'weasel'.

Three Men in a Tub

'Rub a dub dub, three men in a tub,
And who do you think they be?
The butcher,
   the baker,
      the candlestick maker
Turn them out, Knaves all three.'

In 3's walk or swim in small circle.
1 jumps up and drops down under water.
2 repeats.
3 repeats.
All walk, or swim to pool side.

Tipty-toe

'We don't care whether we work or no,
We'll follow our mother on tipty-toe.'

'Mother' crosses pool with children following, walking or swimming forward. When 'mother' turns round suddenly they must be still, or be sent back to starting place at pool side. The 'child' first to touch 'mother' exchanges places.

Paddy from Home

'Paddy from home has never been,
A railway train he's never seen,
He longs to see the great machine
That travels along the railway.'

Line up along shallow end holding elbows of one in front. The 'driver' circles track under tunnel (pair making arch), is held up at a level crossing by cars (swimmers), and pulls up at station to let 'Paddy' get on, and passengers off train. (In and out of pool.)

Ding Dong Bell

'Ding dong bell, pussy's in the well!
Who put her in, little Tommie Green.
Who pulled her out?
Little Janet (Robert, Susan, etc.) Stout.'

Walk or swim in a circle round 'pussy'. The adult calls out one of the children's names, who walks or swims to exchange places with 'pussy'.

Charlie over the Sea

'Charlie over the water,
Charlie over the sea,
Charlie caught a big fish,
But can't catch me.'

Walk, or swim in a circle round 'Charlie'. On 'catch me', 'Charlie' tags as many as possible. Those caught help 'Charlie' to catch others. The last one tagged changes places with 'Charlie'. Repeat using the child's name.

Moonlight, Starlight

'Moonlight, starlight,
The crabs won't come out
                    tonight.'

Three or four 'crabs' in a corner and the others walk, or swim up to them. On 'tonight' 'crabs' tag the rest, who must go to the pool side. The last three or four to be tagged then become 'crabs'.

London's Burning

'London's burning, London's
                    burning,
Fetch the engines, fetch the
                    engines.
Fire! Fire! Fire! Fire!
Pour on water, pour on water.'

Half the group stand making buildings, whilst the other half walk or swim round them. On 'pour on water' latter splash 'London'. Change places.

Bell horses

'Bell horses, bell horses,
What time of day?
1 o'clock, 2 o'clock,
3 and away.'

Partners stand with number 1 in front of number 2 making two circles facing inward. On 'away' the 2's walk or swim in a circle round number 1's, and mount back of partner to see who is first. Change places.

62

Deeper water

Barley Bread

'Mother has called, mother has said
Make haste home and make barley bread.
Up with your heels, down with your head,
This is the way to make barley bread.'

Half the group hold on to the pool side and chant, whilst other half swims.
On 'Up with your heels', surface dive head first, or handstand on pool bottom.
Change places.

Gallant Ship

'Three times round goes the gallant, gallant ship,
And three times round goes she;
Three times round goes the gallant, gallant ship,
And sinks to the bottom of the sea.'

Swim in a small circle once,

twice,

three times.

Surface dive feet first.

Eendy Beendy

'Eendy, Beendy, baniba roe,
Caught a lobster by the toe;
Hopping in the garden, swimming in the sea,
If you want another one, please catch me.'

'Lobsters' tread water, and 'Eendy Beendy' sees how many feet he can touch, with a surface dive.

Three Ships

'I saw three ships come sailing by,	Three joined together swim width.
Come sailing by, come sailing by:	Next three repeat.
I saw three ships come	Next three repeat.
sailing by	Time rhyme to finish when all nine
On Xmas Day in the morning.'	are across width.

Fish Alive

'One, two, three, four, five,	Five swim joined, trying to en-
Once I caught a fish alive;	circle the 'fish', who surface dives
Why did you let him go?	to escape being 'netted'.
Because he bit my finger so.'	

Toss-a-Ball

'Toss-a-ball, toss-a-ball,	Ball throwing, 1 to 2, 2 to 3,
Tell me true,	3 to 4 and 4 to 5,
How many years	5 to 6 and 6 to 7,
I've got to go through?'	7 to 8, 8 to 9, 9 to 10.
	Stand, or tread water.

Simple Simon

'Simple Simon went a-fishing,	Pennies are scattered on pool bot-
For to catch a whale,	tom. Swim to sight position and
And all the water that he had	surface dive once to collect as
Was in his mother's pail.'	many pennies as possible.

Looby

'Here I lie	Horizontal prone float arms be-
The length of a looby,	yond head.
The breadth of a booby,	Star float, legs and arms apart.
And three parts of a jackass.'	Legs together, arms in star posi- tion.

Birds in the Air

'All the birds in the air,
All the fishes in the sea,
Come and pick me out
A brewer or a baker
Or a candlestick maker.'

Hang on with hands and feet to the pool side. Change places along the rail by striding over or ducking under each other. Swim to middle and join right hands with opposite partner, for swimming tug-of-war. A 2- or 3-yard pull denotes the winner.

Turn Cheeses Turn

'Green cheeses, yellow laces,
Up and down the market places;
First a penny then a groat,
Turn, cheeses, turn.'

All swim width or length of pool. Tread water turning round; or spinning top; or water wheel.

Poolside and boards

Frog in the Sea

'Frog in the sea,
Can't catch me.'

All sit or stand on pool side, facing 'frog' in the water. On 'me' all slip, or jump in and walk, or swim across avoiding being caught by 'frog'.

Cuckoo

'Cuckoo in the cherry tree,
Catch a fish and bring it me;
Let the tree be high or low,
Let it hail or rain or snow.'

'Cuckoo' on a diving board, and rest tread water.
'Cuckoo' jumps, or dives, in any direction, to catch one 'fish'.

Jolly Fishermen

'There were three jolly fishermen,
And they all put out to sea,
They cast their nets into the sea,
And three jolly fish caught we.'

Three 'fishermen' stand on pool side, or mount boards of own choice. Jump or dive in to catch one 'fish' each.

E

Ezzeka

'Old Ezzeka did one day stand
Upon a barrel top;
The bung flew out, and all at
           once
It went off with a pop.'

Sit on both sides of pool, change to kneeling, then to standing. One side jumps in with a twist on 'out'. Other side jumps in, holding below knees, to land on seat, on 'pop'.

Libbety-lat

'Libbety, libbety, libbety-lat,
Who can do this?
And who can do that?
And who can do anything?
Better than that?'

In three's to select best trio. One jumps or dives at his own choice. Two repeats from pool side or board. Three repeats. Each trio should try to be different.

Jack be Nimble

'Jack be nimble,
And Jack be quick,
And Jack jump (dive) over
The candlestick.'

One kneels down on the end of 1-metre board, and two stands at other end. Two runs along to jump (dive) over one. Repeat with 3–6 but jump (dive) only on 'jump'.

Three Frogs

'My mistress sent me unto thine,
With three young frogs both
           fair and fine,
And as they here do stand,
Which will you sink
Which will you swim,
And which bring home to land?'

In sixes; three standing on opposite sides of pool.
One jumps (dives) in, and selects a 'frog' who must jump in for tug-of-war.
Two selects for a tandem swim.
Three uses a rescue method for last 'frog'.

CHANTING GAMES

Leaves are Green

The leaves are green, the nuts
                    are brown,
They hang so high they'll not
                 come down;
Leave them alone till frosty
               weather
Then they'll all come down
              together.'

All walk to selected place, on pool side or boards, taking care that they will not obstruct each other. On 'together' jump or dive in.

Ducks and Drakes

'A duck and a drake,
And a halfpenny cake,
And a penny to pay the old
               baker,
A hop and a scotch is another
               notch,
Slitheram, slatherum, take her.'

From side, 1 skims a flat pebble.
    2 repeats, counting bounces.
    3 repeats.

    4 repeats.
Wade, jump, or dive in to recover pebbles, or round discs.

Over the Water

'Over the water at the hour of
               ten,
I'll meet you with five thousand
               men;
Over the water at the hour of
               five,
I'll meet you there if I'm alive.'

Two stand on opposite sides of pool, and the rest tread water. The two dive in trying to meet, while the rest try to prevent it, but without touching them.

GAMES WITHOUT APPARATUS

Shallow water
Horse and jockey
Partners stand facing each other in two rings. At the OFF, inside 'jockeys' surface dive through 'horses' legs, swim round outside of race course, and then mount own horse's back.

Fighting cocks
'Cocks' sit on poolside in shallow end. At signal they mount partner's backs, and a free-for-all ensues until one pair is left.

Snakes and ladders
Half the group are 'ladders' and half 'snakes'. The 'ladders' stand in twos, threes or fours with feet apart, and hands on shoulders of one in front. The 'snakes' swim solo under as many 'ladders' as possible, before whistle blows.

Mr. Shark
All walk or swim after 'Mr. Shark' saying 'What's the time Mr. Shark?' He replies, '5 o'clock', etc., but when he says 'Dinner time', all escape to poolside. Those caught help 'Mr. Shark' in the next game.

Sardines and salmon
Caller on the poolside, with the 'sardine' line in the water back to back with 'salmon'. The caller says 'ssssss sardines', and they then try to reach their own side before being caught by a 'salmon'. Those caught must join other line. Repeat, but not always with an alternate call of 'sardine' or 'salmon'.

Follow the leader
'Leader' performs with a mixture of strokes and skills which the others try to copy.

Deeper water
Blind man's Buff
A small section of the pool only should be used. To give the 'blind man' (swimming cap pulled over eyes) a reasonable chance, the rest swim with a handicap according to ability, such as arms folded; dog paddle; three limbs only or sculling.

Traffic policeman
'Policeman' treads water in middle, and rest are divided between four sides of pool. The 'policeman' directs traffic, so that a cross over, right or left turn is made, with a halt for pedestrians. Examples: fast car (front crawl); lady with dog (breast stroke and dog paddle); motor bike and pillion passenger, or tandem (two waist hold breast stroke); mother with baby in pram (baby floats on back holding mother's shoulders with straight arms, mother breast strokes above); articulated lorry (four waist hold breast stroke); three or four in car, bus etc.

Hampton Court maze
A game for a very large number, who swim in single file following leader round outside of pool, and into smaller and smaller circles until centre is reached. On the signal, all swim out of the maze trying not to be last at the poolside.

GAMES WITH SMALL APPARATUS

Shallow water

Fill and empty

A floating plastic bucket is filled with table tennis or gamester balls. 'He' throws them out singly, and the others must collect and return them quickly, so that the bucket is never empty.

Volley ball

A rope is tied above water across the shallow end. The two teams bat a balloon, or toss a large plastic ball, over the rope. A point is scored if the balloon or ball touches the water.

Aunt Sally

All with a gamester ball stand facing 'Aunt Sally', who stands inside a buoy or inner tube. 'Aunt Sally' dodges the balls by ducking and rising, but if hit changes places with hitter.

Hunt the bellman

All are blindfolded by pulling caps over eyes, except the bellman, who swims and surface dives amongst them, ringing the bell until caught, when he changed places with catcher.

Tug of war

Two hold the end of a broomstick, and either push their opponent backward, or pull him forward, for two or three yards. Alternatively an inner tube can be used.

70

Pair tug of war
Two holding on to either side of broomstick, with breast stroke or crawl kick, try to push the other pair backward. Alternatively they hold the ends of broomstick and swim on their backs, trying to pull the other pair forward.

Rope tug of war
(a) A tied rope with four holding it at each corner with one hand. Each pair tries to pull the other backward, either walking or swimming.
(b) A long rope to which, on alternate sides, canvas loops are tied. Competitors each put a loop over a shoulder and on signal pull backward.

Dice throw
Stand on the poolside and throw two dice. Swim the number of widths indicated on one dice, and use the other to determine the method. Examples: two widths, front crawl legs holding on to float; three widths, sculling head or feet first; five widths, on back.

Dodge ball
Two circles facing each other; those in the outer aim two or three balls at inner. When hit join outer circle. Beginners play in shallow end, but good swimmers should tread water and play in deep end.

Ring ball
Two teams with either a red or blue gamester ball each, and a hoop or inner tube floating midway between them. From the poolside, whilst standing, each team member in turn aims to score by getting the ball into the ring. Score checked by counting red and blue balls in ring. Swim to regain ball.

71

Deeper water
Basketball
Two teams pass a large ball and try to score a goal by hitting the pool end. After each goal the sides change ends.

Cricket
Half on the poolside in line, and half in the water. The bowler stands on the opposite side and bowls underarm in a small pool. To ensure that the ball reaches the batsman in a large pool, the bowler stands on the side at the shallow end and bowls diagonally underarm. The first batsman hits the ball with the flat of the hand, or a small bat if the pool is a large one, to the fielders spread out in the water. He then jumps or dives in and swims widths until the fielders have returned the ball to the bowler. The rest of the batsmen repeat, until all have batted once each. Fielders change with batsmen and try to beat their total score.

Spanish ducats
All swim, and when whistle is blown surface dive and bring up as many pennies as possible.

Number ball
The teams stand on each side of the pool, both numbered 1, 2, 3, 4, etc. The leader stands at the deep end with a large ball which he throws in, and calls out a number. The two contestants with that number jump or dive in, and attempt to get the ball to their side, so scoring their team a point.

Surface diving for plates
About twelve tin plates are thrown into the depth of water

72

most suitable for the swimmers, and not too far apart. Whoever brings up most plates from one surface dive is the winner.

Diving for plates
Repeat, but with one dive from the poolside to collect the plates, instead of a surface dive.

Bombardment
One team divides itself equally on the two sides of the pool, each having a plastic ball. The other team divides itself, half at the shallow end, and half at the deep. The swimmers can start to swim to the other end of the pool any time they like, and the aimers can throw whenever they like. The winning team is the one scoring most direct hits. No underwater swimming is allowed.

Tiddly-winks
All tread water in a circle holding a plastic ball, and in turn try to get it into a floating plastic bucket or bowl.

Parachute landing
Jump off a high board with a parachute (piece of nylon square with a cord at each corner). Swim and surface dive to brick which is on pool bottom, weight down chute with it and leave it on the pool bottom. Surface and escape to shallow end of pool, avoiding enemy fire from bank. According to numbers either against a stop watch, or reaching the shallow end without being hit by plastic balls, by swimming mainly underwater. (See Bombardment.)

Sailors' pigtails
A short black tape tucked into the back and top of girls' costumes, and boys' trunks. Before a signal is given try to 'cut off' (collect) as many pigtails as possible without losing own.

6 · Water Contests

These competitive contests are for stronger swimmers with the exclusive use of a large indoor, or outdoor pool, or suitable open waters. Selections can be made for swimming sports with the addition of some of the methods of crossing the pool from Chapter 4. If possible length races should start at the deep end. The depth for surface dives should be suitable for the ability of the contestants. Sufficient depth and width must be provided for contests which involve falling into the water. The number of 'officials' needed will depend on choice, setting and purpose of contests. When large apparatus is used they must be ready to act like a boxing referee and intervene if necessary.

Solo, width or length
Egg and spoon
Put egg, cork or table tennis ball in spoon. The spoon can be carried either in the hand or the mouth.

Hoop
On the back with hoop held at waist height, and on every stroke the hoop must be passed over head, down the body and under feet in a complete circle.

Lucky number
Draw for numbers, and numbered tin plates are dropped into the deep end. Race from shallow end, surface dive with eyes open to recover own numbered plate, and deliver it to poolside.

Arms only
Swim on back or front using arms only, keeping a float between knees.

Broken arm
With one arm in wrist and neck sling, swim on back or side stroke.

Pancake day
Swim with frypan, toss and catch in it a small flat yellow disk three or more times, without dropping it into the water.

Brick recovery
Swim, surface dive to recover brick, swim on back supporting brick on chest with both hands and place it on poolside.

Clothing carry
Swim holding clothes wrapped in towel on head, without getting bundle wet.

Row your boat
Sit in an inner tube and using arms like oars row backward.

Paddle boat
Prone on air bed, either paddle forward with arms alternately, or simultaneously.

Fins
Either front or back crawl wearing fins, or front or back paddle without using arms.

Stormy weather
Either swim with an open umbrella, or open and close it a given number of times.

Comic cuts
Either read one page of comic and be able to say what it is about, or finish the distance without getting comic wet.

Solo, there and back
Beaker
Swim width and take plastic beaker from poolside, fill it with water and swim back without spilling it.

Goodnight
Swim width wearing pyjamas and either carry back a lighted candle, or fill a hot-water bottle with pool water. Alternatively a four-width race with candle and bottle can be staged, or the candle carried in one hand and bottle in the other, on the return journey.

Geisha
Swim width, either climb out or hang on to poolside and make a paper fan, swim back fanning, keeping the fan dry.

Polo
Swim width, pick up ball and dribble it back between front crawl arms.

Paris model
Swim width and either climb out, hang on to, or stand at poolside. Make a paper hat from a sheet of newspaper, swim back wearing it.

Deportment
Draw for numbers, swim width and find own numbered plate on poolside. Swim back with tin plate balanced on head.

76

Balloon
Swim width, blow up balloon and nose it back to starting place.

Solo, collecting objects
Fishing
With a fishing net collect six floating corks and deliver at shallow end.

Cafeteria
Collect a floating plastic tray, cup and saucer, surface dive for metal spoon, and deliver completed 'order' at shallow end.

Threading beads
Thread six floating gamester balls on to a cord, and finish at shallow end wearing 'necklace'.

Pearl divers
Wearing face mask and carrying plastic bag, surface dive to pick up six small objects, and try to be first at poolside with 'pearls' in pouch.

Bottle message
Pick up a floating plastic lemonade bottle, extract and read the message, and repeat it at the shallow end.

Bangles
Collect two or more floating quoits, and finish wearing 'bangles' round wrists.

Pairs, without apparatus, widths or lengths
Tandem
Using any linkage.

77

Rescue
Any method of towing.

Blindfold rescue
Rescuer pulls cap over eyes, and rescues partner who gives directions to avoid collision with others, whilst crossing pool once.

Dr. Livingstone
Swim from opposite ends to meet in the middle and shake hands. (Dr. Livingstone, I presume?) With right hands joined swim to shallow end.

Loch Ness Monster
Number 2 holds on to an ankle of number 1, and so joined the pair undulate across the width.

Pairs, with apparatus, widths or lengths
Nurse and baby
'Nurse' pushes or pulls 'baby' in inner tube, or on airbed.

Needle threading
Swim from opposite ends, one with a blunt embroidery needle stuck into a cork, the other with a piece of thread. Stand or tread water in the middle, threading needle, and both swim to shallow end with cork.

Ball exchange
Number 1 swims across with ball held between legs. Number 2 dribbles it between arms for second width.

Pyjama game
Number 1 swims across with pyjamas, without getting them

wet, to number 2 standing on the poolside. Number 2 puts pyjamas on, jumps or dives in for second width.

Hoop and brick
Hoop loosely tied to brick, pair swim from opposite ends and both surface dive through hoop, then detach it from brick. Number 1 rescues brick on the chest to shallow end, number 2 solo hoop races to the deep end.

Threes, widths or lengths
Back rescue
On backs, number 1 grasps number 2's right elbow with right hand, whilst supporting head with left hand. Number 3 grasps number 2's left arm, and 1 and 3 swim head first backward rescuing 2, with or without fins.

Front rescue
Numbers 1 and 3 face downward, number 2 faces upward. The rescuers grasp number 2 under the armpit with inside hand, and hold wrist with outside hand, with or without fins.

Double rescue
All on backs, number 2 (very strong swimmer) tows numbers 1 and 3 by their chins.

Free lift
In file, numbers 1 and 3 swim breast stroke supporting number 2, who holds number 1's shoulders with hands, whilst feet are on either side of number 3's neck.

Liquorice all sorts, price 6p
Each swims two widths using two methods, making a total of six different ways of crossing the pool.

Fours, widths or lengths
Boatrace
Teams of four swim joined, the easiest way is usually the back stroke, but breast stroke can also be used.

Rope rescue
File of four stand in shallow end. Number 1 swims to the side, gets out and throws the end of a rope to number 2, who is then pulled in to the side to repeat with number 3, who repeats with number 4. All finish on poolside.

Miners' race
Three stand astride in file in shallow end, facing number 1 who is on the poolside holding an underwater torch. Number 1 dives along tunnel with torch switched on, to end of file. Torch is passed along to number 2, who swims with it to get out. File moves up one place to repeat.

Relay/Medley
Either four swimmers use fastest strokes, or medley relay with back crawl, breast stroke, butterfly and front crawl.

Fin race
A pair of fins which will fit all four team members. Number 1 fins to 2 and hands fins over, 2 to 3, and 3 to 4.

Large apparatus contests
A large clock, easily seen by competitors and spectators, is needed for 'against the clock' contests.

A. PLANKS, SUPPORTED ON STANDS ON POOL BOTTOM, OR FLOATING SUPPORTS
Solo
Walk backward; forward on all fours; hop; bounce, throw

or roll a ball; step through hoop and circle over head; stilt walk; pogo stick; small cycle.

Pairs
Wrestle in middle; pick-a-back; 1 holds 2 in wheelbarrow position; ball throw and catch from poolside to middle walking forward; repeat from middle to side walking backward; 1 pushes 2 in a wheelbarrow. (*Plate 8a.*)

Threes and Fours
1 and 2 carry 3, with invalid chair linkage; 1 leads blindfolded 2, 3 and 4 across planks. Competitors not eliminated by falling in can compete 'against the clock'.

B. WOODEN RAFT
Mop fight
Stand on raft, and try to push opponent into water using the mop head, but only below shoulder level.

Fig. 2. Mop Fight

King of the Castle
Minimum of four stand on raft, on signal a free for all ensues until only one remains.

C. SHORT ROUND POLE SUPPORTED ON CROSS-BARS ON POOL BOTTOM
Tightrope
Balance walk across pole holding open umbrella.

Pillow fight
Sit astride pole, and try to dislodge opponent with two balloons in a polythene bag.

D. SMALL METAL OR WOODEN BARREL
Barrel balance
Mount barrel, and propel across width on it.

Jousting
Astride barrel, try to dislodge opponent with two balloons in a polythene bag tied to a stick.

E. RUBBER DINGHIES, OR SMALL LIGHTWEIGHT BOATS
Naval battle
Two dinghies with crew armed with two balloons in a poly-

Fig. 3. Naval Battle

thene bag. Battle is not won until a dinghy's whole crew is in the water. Whilst a crew member is still in a dinghy the battle can continue, with the others joining in from the water, trying to upset the enemy dinghy.

Viking raid
'Eric the Red' versus 'Alec the Green', paddling with fry-pans or saucepans, trying to land first on enemy territory. *Plate 8 b.*

F. CANVAS STRETCHER, LIFEBUOYS OR INNER TUBES
Stretcher race
At shallow end, numbers 1 and 2 put number 3 on stretcher on poolside, transfer stretcher on to lifebuoys or inner tubes. Pull or push across pool to land casualty *safely* on stretcher on opposite side of pool.

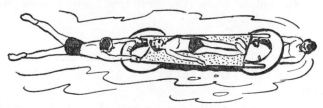
Fig. 4. Stretcher Race

G. LIGHTWEIGHT TENTS ERECTED ON GRASS
Tent transport
Minimum of two tents, each dismantled by a team of three or four, transported across pool and back. Re-erected with the tent still *dry*.

H. MONO-RAIL WITH STEEL CABLE TO HOOK ON TO
   DIVING BOARD, WALL, POSTS OR TREES
Splash down
Hold handlebars and travel supported on pulley until over

Fig. 5. Splash Down

target, then splash down, aiming to land inside large floating hoop, or inner tube.

I. CANOE, POSTS (WATER POLO), BRIDGES, OVERHANGING AND FLOATING OBSTACLES
Slalom
Canoe is paddled round set course of obstacles 'against clock'.

J. CHUTE, AIRBEDS, RUBBER GYMNASTIC MATS
Solo Cresta run
Slide down chute on to airbed, and propel it a set distance by own choice of method, 'against clock'.

Partner Cresta run
Number 1 slides down chute on to rubber gymnastic mat, and keeps it under chute for number 2 to land on. Pair propel it a set distance by own choice of method, 'against clock'.

Push off!
Three sit on rubber gymnastic mat, and on signal try to push each other off it. *Plate 2b.*

Solo, place in the sun
Reclining on back on airbeds, plus one extra competitor. On signal roll off bed and swim until next signal, when everyone tries to claim a bed. Eliminated competitor removes a bed, until only the winner has earned a 'place in the sun'.

Pair, place in the sun
Repeat in pairs on rubber gymnastic mats, with two extra competitors.

K. SCRAMBLING NET, ROPES, ROPE LADDERS SUSPENDED FROM DIVING BOARDS

Assault course
Individuals, or small teams, from shallow end propel on barrels or inner tubes, round poles and slalom obstacles, dismount and climb over and swim under other obstacles. Finish by climbing up rope fixture to finish on diving board, 'against clock'.

Commando
Swimmers individually cover an assault course against a stop watch, to see who has the fastest time. Example— Jump or dive in from a high board. Swim over, under or round various obstacles. Surface dive and pick up objects, and put them in different places. Climb out at the deep end, up a suspended rope or ladder, to finish on a diving board. Alternatively can be, 'against clock'.

L. INNER TUBES TIED ON ALTERNATE SIDES OF RACING LANE ROPE

Musical chairs

Competitors swim clockwise non-stop, diving over or ducking under the rope lane at each end of the pool. When the music stops, competitors sit in an inner tube. Eliminated competitor unties a tube, but leaves those at the top and bottom of the rope. Repeat until only one pair is left, with an equal chance of reaching the top and bottom 'chair' first.

Cavalry charge

The opposing armies sit or lie on an inner tube, and on the signal all propel themselves forward to meet the enemy. A free-for-all ensues, and the victors are those with the fewest dislodged casualties.

M. HOOPS FLOATING ON SURFACE

Jack in the box

One hoop fewer than the competitors, who swim clockwise on the outside of the pool. On the signal a hoop is claimed by ducking under it, and kicking upward to raise head and shoulders through it. Eliminated competitor removes a hoop, until only a pair is left. These two have an equal chance of becoming 'Jack in the Box' in the remaining hoop.

N. LONG AND SHORT ROPES, DEFLATED FOOTBALL, RING OR QUOIT

Punch ball

A strong rope is stretched across the pool. A partially deflated football hangs on a short thin rope from it, on a sliding ring or quoit, and about one foot from the surface. Two teams either stand, or swim on each side of the rope. A goal is scored by punching the ball until it reaches the left-hand side of the pool. In a small pool the rope would be lengthwise, with goals at the deep and shallow ends, and teams would change sides after a goal is scored. The latter would not be necessary in a shallow learner pool, as all team members would be standing throughout.

O. LARGE MAP DRAWN ON BLACKBOARD
Sunken treasure
The map is studied showing where the treasure ship may lie, but no starting point is given. The instructions will vary according to the pool and ability of swimmers. Example: four strokes forward, surface dive; five strokes forward underwater; surface; turn sharp right; ten strokes backward, surface dive feet first; four strokes underwater sideways left; surface and tread water when over the sunken treasure. The winner is the one nearest to the 'treasure' spot decided upon by the leader.

Fun and games contests can also be enjoyed on, and in, open waters, if due precautions are taken. Plate 7.

7 · Water Shows

This chapter aims to give ideas for the entertainment of spectators by performers, who have the necessary skill and will enjoy the training involved. Sufficient dry land personnel and experts must be available for the necessary hard work which will ensure success.

COMPOSITIONS

The age, sex and ability of the swimmers, plus the size of pool and space available round it, will determine what will make a successful water show. Properties which take up needless spectator space, or obscure their view, or swimmers so costumed that their swimming is hampered, will result in an end product in which the actual swimming has suffered. However, I believe there is a place for a water show in school, club and family or party programmes; so long as the standard is high.

I instance three Primary School compositions: in the first place it will be noted that there were many 'dry land' performers taking part. When the swimmers can be separated from the latter, the costuming is made easier. Electronic music, or other appropriate instruments can be played; singing or choral speech can be used as an accompaniment.

Moses in the bulrushes
Record: 'Exodus'. Recorders: March from *Aida*.
    'She took for him a basket made of bulrushes; . . . and she

put the child in it and placed it among the reeds at the river's brink.'

EXODUS 11, 3

Starting position: Rings of floaters wearing flowered caps, holding plastic flower-covered hoops. Low diving board covered with reeds and weighted greenery. Moses' mother and sister creep in carrying Moses in a basket—lightened by polystyrene floats. The sister slips into the water, receives the basket, and swims to secure it in the rushes, and returns. The pair hide as a procession is heard approaching. Dancers enter followed by Pharaoh's daughter carried on a litter (carpet-covered top of gymnastic box). Slaves are commanded to collect flowers from the Nile. They float, and surface-dive to emerge in the centre of a hoop of flowers, or somersault backward to surface inside or beside a hoop. According to their ability they perform other skills until all the flowered hoops have been collected from the floaters. Moses' basket is discovered and is swum to the side and handed to Pharaoh's daughter. Moses' sister creeps out of hiding and offers to get a nurse, and his mother is brought forward. The procession re-forms, with recorders leading, and moves to exit. Plates 5 a and b.

Lines and circles

Record: H.M.V. 'Wheels-Cha-Cha', Joe Loss.

Starting position: Numbered 1–8 at the deep end, close together in half-kneeling position, left-hand side of pool viewing from shallow end.

A. Number 1, half-kneeling dives in and swims width breast stroke, followed in turn by 2–8. Hold rail with right hand.

B. Number 1 swims width breast stroke, followed in turn by 2–8. Hold rail with left hand.

89

C. Number 1 leads file into large clockwise circle on breast stroke.
D. Numbers 1 and 5 lead into two clockwise circles in line down pool, on breast stroke.
E. Divide into four clockwise circles holding partner's right shoulder for *water-wheel*, in line down pool.
F. Number 1 leads file on breast stroke to deep end, climb out and line up on poolside.

Frogmans' frolic
Record: 'Entry of the Gladiators'.
Starting Position: Boys numbered 1–6 in file, all wearing fins.

Flap march round pool to line up in pairs on side at deep end. Enter water in turn by own choice of pair method: jump, pick-a-back, sitting or standing dive. In turn fin to deep end and hold rail.

Odd numbers fin half-way down pool, surface dive waggling fins.

Even numbers repeat, all finish standing at shallow end.

Odd numbers fin forward, stand and part legs for even numbers to surface dive through, waggling fins.

Even numbers repeat—in shallow pool continue whole length, otherwise continue until water is too deep to stand, but finish at deep end.

Odd numbers fin to shallow end, handstand on pool bottom waggling fins.

Even numbers repeat. Both repeat, line up standing at shallow end. Number 1 leads, followed in turn by 2–6 finning to deep end. Climb out, stand to attention. Turn right and flap march exit. (*Plates 4a and b*)

Ideas for compositions for water shows can be derived from very many sources—nursery rhymes; myths and legends; stories; poetry; art; music; nature; history; geography; science and humour.

If spectator space is limited then 'dry land' performers could be replaced by other water users. Suitably decorated canoes and small craft could be incorporated as required.

Water craft could produce a Carnival or Water Pageant on their own. The latter might even be staged on inland waters, with plenty of space for themes such as 'Merrie England', or A.D. '2000'. This would involve a colourful procession of gaily decorated boats.

Sub-aquanauts could also make a contribution in suitable compositions. Alternatively the sub-aqua group could produce their own UNDERWATER SHOW. This could be both educational and entertaining, as was a Police Underwater Unit's demonstration of training procedures, followed by the assembling of a bicycle under water and then riding it.

FIGURE FLOATING

If the supported floating has been enjoyed, then figure floating could be the next step. The services of a coach should be sought, and if a skilful performance results, the preparation of a display item might be considered.

Grips
All grips should be stable, uniform and from beneath to give upward pressure whenever possible. Grips not illustrated, but which should be tried, are elbow, shoulder and back of waist grasp.

Grips with hands
Hand clasp = A, N, P, R.
Overgrasp wrist = O, M, Q.

Instep grasp = B, D, E, H, I, J, K, Q.
Ankle grasp = F, G.

Grips with legs
Interlock legs below knee = C.
Interlock ankles = Q, R.
Interlock arms with legs = D, H.
Neck grasp with feet = H, L, M.
Pair foot grasp = O, Q.

Hand Clasp

Overgrasp Wrist

Instep Grasp

Ankle Grasp

Interlock Legs

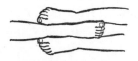

Interlock Ankles

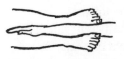

Interlock Arms with Legs

Neck Grasp   One Foot on top   Pair Foot Grasp
                    other underneath

Change position by sculling = C, D, H.
Travel backward by sculling = M.
Travel backward by opening and closing arms and legs = J.
Travel backward by moving arms = L.
Move circle counter clockwise by strongly closing right leg
   to left = P.
Middle two floaters bend outside knee = G.
Bend right knee, open and close legs, bend left knee, and
   repeat = N, P.
Maintain floating position = O, Q, R.

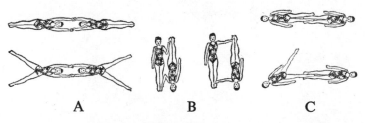

Fig. 6. Floating—Pairs

93

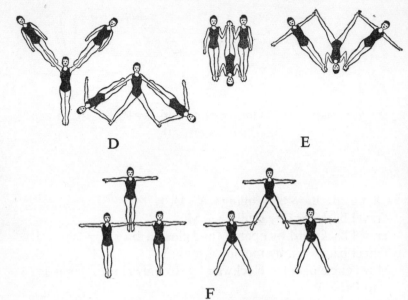

D   E

F

Fig. 7. Floating—Threes

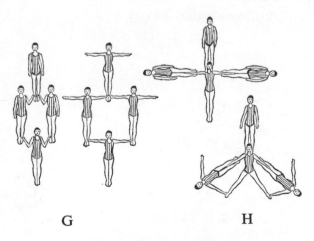

G   H

Fig. 8. Floating—Fours

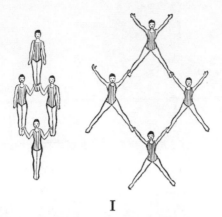

I

Fig 8. Floating—Fours—Continued.

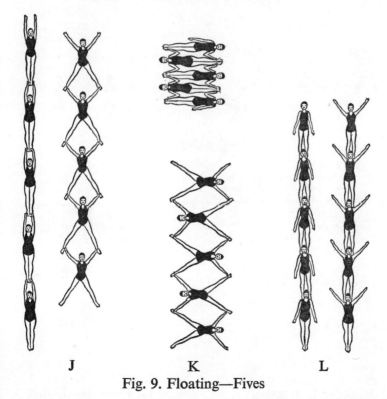

J   K   L

Fig. 9. Floating—Fives

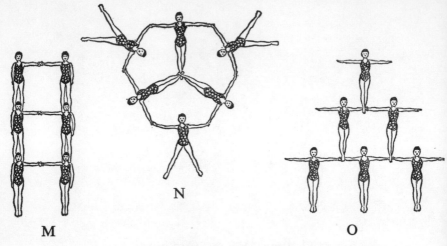

Fig. 10. Floating—Sixes

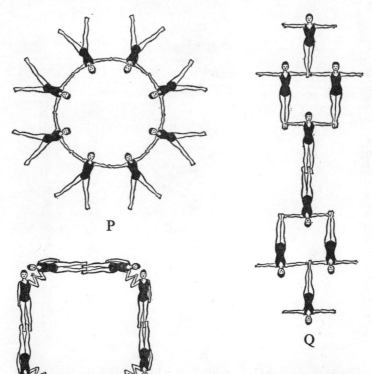

Fig. 11. Floating—Eights

Hints

Try out the figures on land, then in shallow water, with assistance from supports if necessary. Have someone on the poolside to coach, and provide the signals on which to move. The latter can be by voice, whistle, hand or stick clap, drum beat or some other form of percussion. Working as a unit, the floaters 'on cue' should move slowly and accurately, to arrive in the correct position. If music, or a definite time factor, is to follow later, then 'counting or beating cues' will be needed.

Start simply by working in pairs, and experiment with figures other than those illustrated. In this way it is possible to add to your repertoire in many ways, and incidentally discover which figures can be performed by the group. The latter will be dependent on the overall ability and numbers available, plus reserves. As each floater has to keep her body as straight as possible, curved shapes can be achieved only by having sufficient numbers. An example of this is floating to form letters of the alphabet, as in the CLUB INITIALS FLOAT.

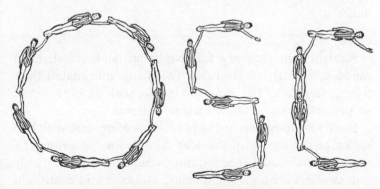

Fig. 12. Club Initials Float

Swim into the starting position from different places all round the poolside, or diagonally from one side of the pool. Assume the floating position, and hold it without fuss, fidgeting or sinking. On the signal move slowly from figure to figure, arriving on time if counting is used. On conclusion scull or back paddle to poolside.

STROKE PATTERNS

We all enjoy the precision marching seen in a Tattoo, and the same effect can be achieved by a minimum of four swimmers, willing to practise regularly together. The strokes used can be breast, back, side, front and back crawl, waltz, i.e. combined front and back crawl. The patterns can be achieved on only one stroke, or a combination of strokes; with fast or slow time, or a combination of times. The ability of all the swimmers is the deciding factor on ultimate choice, as team precision is essential. Exclude a really weak swimmer, a good swimmer who lacks the necessary stamina to keep up and the individual, who for one reason or another, is not team minded.

Correct spacing must be maintained and strokes must be uniform.

EXAMPLES

Straight arm recovery for front and back crawl, head raised sufficiently to see other swimmers, and match their timing, feet under the water, no splash, sculling as required, so presenting seemingly effortless patterns.

Start with someone on the poolside beating time with two sticks, or a drum, until the beat suitable for the swimmers' stroke is established. The swimmers can begin by using only one stroke with uniform spacing, swimming in a straight line keeping time with the beat. If large numbers can participate the possible permutations are endless.

EXAMPLES

Line abreast, turn about and swim through gaps; single file, alternate dividing off into two's, then four's; weaving across the pool; diagonal crossing from pool corners to swim through gaps; small and large circles; combined circles and lines.

Do not be too ambitious, but work out a simple pattern on paper. Then try out the patterns on land, with attention paid to spacing and time keeping. Experiment, adjust and discard in the water, until you are satisfied with the result. Music, with a regular beat, can then be selected to fit your pattern making. You might find that a battery record player is the safest, unless the pool has correctly installed electrical sound equipment. Later you could choose the music first, and fit the patterns to it, perhaps progressing to tempo and stroke changes. Progressions can continue indefinitely, even to the extent of using pair linkage, such as tandem breast stroke and sculling in two's.

FIGURE FORMATION TEAM

A combination of figure floating and stroke patterns can make an effective and enjoyable display item, especially viewed from raised seating, or balcony. A short simple number, well within the capabilities of the performers, should be the aim. Four good swimmers will make a better team than eight mediocre ones, and reserves will need to practise as well. Practices should start in good time, but not so early that a mechanical and stale performance results. The display should be incidental, and the work varied to be truly enjoyed by the whole group. The team will need to find extra time for the final practices. The music chosen should not be hackneyed, and a *Top of the Pops* tune might be outdated by the time the display is given. Have at least two records, if the music is not to be taped. The person in charge should have worked with the team throughout, and be capable of dealing with plugs, extra cabling and any emergency as it arises during the item itself! Costumes should be neat, workmanlike, minus zip fasteners, and chosen to suit all team members, and the tune. Caps, which could be suitably decorated, should be worn so that hair does not obscure vision, leading to lack of precision. Long toe and finger-nails (best unvarnished), use of sun tan oil, and the wearing of jewellery, could also make it difficult to maintain a team spirit! Nose clips may need to be worn by some swimmers. Use should be made of lines on the pool bottom and ceiling, and spots earmarked on the walls to help maintain timing and spacing.

DISPLAYS AND DEMONSTRATIONS

The Monte Christo Sack Trick can be most effective. A large sack, weighted with two or three rubber bricks, and with a hole cut out at the top for the rope is needed. The swimmer

Fig. 13. Monte Christo Sack Trick

holds the loosened ends of the doubled rope, and grips the nearby sacking. The assistant ties the rope ends on the opposite side from the hole. On signal, the swimmer takes a deep breath before being thrown into the water, and sinks feet first because of the bricks. The swimmer releases his rope ends, and swims upward out of the open sack.

The Figure Formation Team can invite spectators to throw money on to their club's flag or decorated sheet, and then surface dive or backward somersault for the 'near misses'. Alternatively they can begin with stroke patterns,

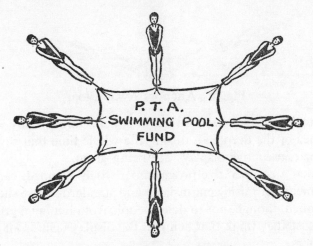

Fig. 14. Club Collecting Float

and culminate with the anchor float to the tune, *Anchors Away*. If there are suitable diving boards, a comedy turn using buckets, watering-cans and planks tied on to ropes can be staged.

The local life saving group can unexpectedly simulate a realistic-looking emergency. However, the 'rescuer' has to be quick off the mark, or he can be beaten to it by an eager beaver spectator! 'Drownproofing' requires time to demon-

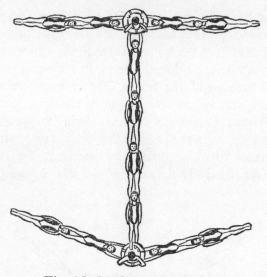

Fig. 15. Anchors Away Float

strate its effectiveness, so its exponents are usually in a corner of the deep end, during the whole time that several other consecutive displays are being given.

Such a co-operative programme, wisely planned, can be the means of raising enthusiasm and standards. Care should be taken, though, not to deter people from joining a group, because they think that being in the display team is all that matters.

Experts can be invited to give demonstrations of swimming; diving; synchronized swimming; and surf board routines. For water polo, sub-aqua and life-saving, the help of club, college or police teams can be sought. A 'Salmon Run' makes a good finale for a water show. For this all the swimmers line up at the deep end and cruise down the pool in successive waves. Displays and demonstrations need an announcer with a clear delivery, used to a microphone, but able to cope if it breaks down (a whistle is a good standby).

Fig. 16. Surf Board Display

He should be able to pin-point the highlights, obtain silence when required, but in a pleasant and non-hectoring manner. He should also be able to *ad lib* if there is an unexpected hold up.

At a Water Fête a link could be made with other displays and demonstrations. If the pool is a new one, serving a wide area of non-swimmers, the displays and demonstrations could be mounted accordingly. They might include material obtained from the Royal Society for the Prevention of Accidents, the Royal Life Saving Society, the Amateur Swimming Association; and general information on the classes and groups meeting in the pool. A pool used for sub-aqua and canoe training could have exhibitions showing the work of the British Sub-Aqua Club and the British Canoe Union and Canoe Camping Club. It is useful if different bodies undertake responsibility for various jobs, such as the catering, litter disposal, the crèche, heavy work and transport.

103

8 · Where

OPEN WATERS

If swimming is to be fully and widely enjoyed as a recreation for all ages, we must be made more aware of the need for better facilities and for their more imaginative use.

The sea is perhaps the most obvious place to swim. However, in Great Britain, though a competent swimmer can revel in the waves and even enjoy the cold, it is far too large and unfamiliar a setting to enable a young child to learn to swim easily. He may paddle at the edge happily enough, but if he is carried into deep water for an unwanted swimming lesson then water may become something to be feared permanently. Full use of the sea is also prevented in very many areas by pollution from oil, chemicals and sewage.

Pollution also prevents the full use of inland waters; rivers, pools and lakes. In urban areas the causes are mainly industrial waste, sewage and detergent foam, and even rural waters may be polluted by chemical fertilizers and waste from intensively reared animals. In my father's day the European Distance Championships were held in the Thames, Seine, Meuse, Danube and Rhine. The pollution content of the Rhine is now 10–15 units per cubic metre at Basle; 2,000 units at Strasbourg and 1,500,000 units at Rotterdam. Those who fall into such rivers are taken immediately to hospital and stomach-pumped. This problem is shared by all European countries, and its solution must be sought as leisure pursuits make ever-increasing demands on the world's water resources. The rewards of success will be enormous, as anyone who can still enjoy unpolluted open waters will realize.

SWIMMING BATHS

The Greeks were the first to build baths, and the Romans the first to cover them. We might well compare our own provision of baths with theirs. At one time there were no fewer than 850 baths in Rome and its environs, many of them luxuriously furnished with marble, mosaics and frescoes. Some of them could accommodate a thousand people and provided hot, cold, tepid, vapour and swimming baths as well as gymnasia, lecture rooms and halls. They were open long hours and the admission charges could be afforded by even the poorest Roman.

In Britian today swimming pools are provided by many different bodies and organizations. Everyone who is interested in swimming should concern themselves with the wider provision of pools and with the fuller realization of the potentialities of existing facilities.

LOCAL AUTHORITY POOLS

Steady but slow progress has been made since Liverpool Corporation opened a bath in 1828. In 1846 an Act of Parliament was passed to promote the establishment of baths and washhouses, and London had seven baths in 1852. But it is only recently that the provision of baths is again seen as a matter of urgency.

Though Sunday opening is becoming more general, many existing baths still offer only limited and unimaginative facilities, often closing down in the winter to raise money by staging wrestling matches and other more profitable activities. A much more satisfactory solution to financial problems would be to make the pools more inviting and challenging for a wider age and ability range. The pools could be used for training for other sports and a new sport, which I would call Aquabatics, might be introduced, but all this would require programmed pool usage. It is almost impossible for both recreative and competitive swimmers to enjoy a swim at the same time, and public sessions are often too noisy, crowded and boisterous for the nervous swimmer, the learner and for mothers with small children. Programmed sessions might include periods for parents and small children; for older children and teenagers; for survival and life-saving; for competitive swimming; for the handicapped; for water sports, as well as for the usual general public's recreative swimming. Special equipment could be provided for Aquabatic sessions in existing indoor pools; portable climbing frames, for example, to rest on the pool bottom, for climbing, swimming through, and for jumping and diving off; trapeze, ropes, rope ladders and climbing nets could be attached to diving boards or hung across the pool. See IN AND OUT, Chapter 9.

There are even more exciting possibilities for existing large outdoor pools. Those with more than one chute could

Fig. 17. Trapeze Somersault

have the tallest adapted to take toboggans. Helter-skelter towers could be sited to land in the water. Wave-making machinery could be supplied for canoeing, sailing and surfing; a water ski-ing simulator; and portable obstacles on the pool bottom for sub-aquanauts. The season could be extended by installing ice-making machinery for skating, curling and ice-hockey. On the pool side stone picnic/table tennis tables, ground draughts, chess and shuffle board, trampolines, climbing apparatus, seesaw, slides, swings and sand pits would widen the appeal of the pool for all ages.

New pools, too, could profit from a more imaginative approach. Many of these are a vast improvement, sometimes being part of a larger recreative complex, where different members of a family can share transport and then follow their chosen leisure pursuit. Many are now built to 'Olympic' standards, with a small 'learner' pool. The latter should have steps along the whole of one end for the disabled, as well as for learners, and could incorporate special entrance facilities for the former. Many new pools could be improved by programmed pool usage, and could incorporate features which would facilitate teaching, improve safety training and increase the recreational opportunities.

An adjustable pool floor with a water depth to suit the programmed sessions or movable barriers which divided the pool into separate water spaces, would make it easier to use the pool for group instruction. Tip-up seats on the poolside for swimmers and blackboards for teachers and coaches would fill a need. Underwater observation windows and lighting would be a help in training and demonstrating. There should also be a lecture/club room, with visual aids for training competitive swimmers, divers and participants in other water sports, and a 'Kiss of Life' manikin for regular demonstrations. Gymnastic apparatus could be fixed to the walls or ceiling and pulled into position for

Aquabatics. A public address and an amplification system for music, and if possible a soundproof room for testing synchro equipment would be valuable. A refreshment room is essential and should overlook the pool. Also needed are private baths and showers, both for local use and for visitors to the town, and special dressing and toilet facilities for handicapped swimmers. Warm-air drying facilities and Sauna suites could also be incorporated. Saunas have proved to be a source of increased revenue, as have the hairdressing salons. Weighing machines should be provided.

Local Authorities usually provide paddling pools for small children. Many are far too shallow to allow children to lie down and be fully covered by the water. If these were deepened, or built with a deep end, children could become used to the horizontal swimming position and acquire water confidence much earlier.

SCHOOL POOLS

Many large schools now have their own swimming pool. We must aim for a brighter future. This is an absolute necessity as today half the school leavers are unable to swim, having received insufficient or no instruction.

The English School's Swimming Association launched an admirable scheme with the catch phrase: 'Every school a pool'. Parent-Teacher Associations built many pools, mainly of the outdoor learner type. Unfortunately, later on some of these pools proved costly to maintain, and some even failed to pass the examination of the Medical Officer of Health. Since those early days the pool building industry has become large and well organized. With outdoor pools the present trend is to buy the pool itself, and perhaps cut down on costs by using the voluntary labour of parents, teachers and pupils for paving, terracing, seat building and fencing. Some kind of fencing is usually necessary as a safety measure, wind-break and, with an awning, to give some protection to the teacher. Pupils enjoy a lesson in the rain, but the teacher may have to spend several lessons in it! If foundations are dug for the pool the soil can provide a bank, and this makes an ideal viewpoint. Sufficient spectator space should always be left between the pool and fencing, as in a very short space of time the opening ceremony, swimming sports and displays will almost certainly be held.

Pool Committees should phase their expenditure and hasten slowly, if by so doing they eventually have a better pool. The first phase would be filtration, chlorination, heating, diving board, changing rooms and all the amenities which make a communal recreative facility, rather than a small learner school pool. The warmth of a heated pool, with its extended season, achieves results which bear no comparison with unheated pools. There is an American saying, 'An unheated pool is only a tub of cold water' and swimming is not easily learnt in cold water. The Americans had their pools heated between 80° F. and 90° F. when ours were 72° F. or less. Today indoor learner pools are often 82° F. or more, and swimmers' pools 76° F. to 84° F. Roofing can be left until the second stage unless the pool is in a grimy area with air pollution. The roof should be attractive and retain the pool's natural look, so that on a summer's day it is as pleasant as an outdoor pool.

A pool serving a local area is useful as every school cannot have its own pool. This can probably be used by a group of neighbouring schools during school hours. After school, at weekends and during holidays it can be used for organized play leadership schemes, youth groups, clubs and classes for non-swimmers, survival, life saving, display teams, sub-aqua, but not by individual swimmers. Separate access to the pool and changing facilities are needed when the pool is on a school site.

Approval for a school pool, and its siting, has to be obtained from the Local Education Authority, if it is a state school. Private schools should check with the Town and Country Planning Departments. Architects and Planning Departments are quite rightly concerned that a pool should fit in with its surroundings aesthetically, and this is essential if it is to be an indoor pool. As the L.E.A. will maintain the pool if it is built on their property, they will need to be satisfied that the workmanship is not sub-standard, resulting in a liability after a few years. A grant from the L.E.A. can be sought by the Pool Committee.

The size and depth of a pool will depend on its users, the site and money available. Recommendations can be obtained from the Association of Swimming Pool Contractors; Institute of Baths Management; Amateur Swimming Association; English Schools' Swimming Association and Ministry of Education and Science. I would suggest that, when possible, a learner pool is 12·5 m. × 7 m., with a 2′ 6″, 2′ 9″ or 3′ 0″ overall depth, according to the height of the children, with shallow steps leading down from one end or side. On the other three sides, instead of a scum trough, there should be a teaching rail suitable for the children's grip, and *at water level*. For the indoor all-purpose pool the measurements should be *at least* 20 m. × 8 m.; with 2′ 9″ or 3′ to 6′ 6″ for diving from the side, or 2′ 9″ or 3′ to 8′ 6″ for a one-metre board. Lengths and widths should be metric.

Free standing learner pools have been erected in basements, corridors and empty classrooms. They are usually of the 'liner' type with sectional walls which can be tailored to fit the space available. Re-siting of electric fittings is sometimes necessary, plus means of dealing with condensation.

Some schools maintain such strict timetabling that pupils

are rushed in and out of the water. This can mean insufficient time to visit the lavatory and to dry properly. The hygienic use of school pools is essential, as it is here that the foundation is laid of respect for the proper use of public pool facilities. School pools have been known to be used for a 'clean up' immediately after a game of rugby!

SPECIAL SCHOOL POOLS

In the past swimming pools, as well as hydrotherapy pools, have been specially designed for the sole use of handicapped pupils. This may be because specially built-in features were needed, such as ramps or hydraulic lifts to enter and leave the water. Many Parent/Teacher Associations and charitable bodies have provided these pools. Swimming is a wonderful sport for the handicapped, and as they make measurable progress, they thereby derive pleasure and confidence. This is a joy for those teaching them and an inspiration for all of us. However, it is very easy to underestimate their ability, courage and determination, and to build a pool accordingly. Very many handicapped pupils who have wanted to accept the challenge of trying to gain the various swimming awards have been prevented by the design of their pool. A more suitable pool might be built with thoughtful initial planning, and guidance sought from such bodies as the Association of Swimming Therapy. The latter could also advise on teaching techniques, and the Swimming Teachers' Association have a Supplementary Certificate for the Teaching of the Handicapped to Swim.

Special School Pools might be used by other people occasionally, as swimming water heated to a temperature of 85° F. to 90° F. is far too precious a commodity to lie idle. It is known that some handicapped pupils may be inconti-

111

nent. However, extra special care is taken in these schools, and no children swim at risk to themselves and others. The lavatories, showers and footbaths are used and special rubber pants worn if necessary. Handicapped pupils have more adult help and supervision, and so are probably amongst the most hygienic of all pool users. When approached a blind school was very willing for classes from the mental hospital to use its excellently designed pool. Another pool with a ramp in it was willingly made available to a 'Mother and Baby' class, for which it was ideal. A Junior Training Centre's learner pool was used for adult learners in the evenings. This sharing of facilities can lead to mutual benefit of many different kinds.

Reference book:

Teaching the Physically Handicapped to Swim, William Anderson (Faber and Faber Ltd.).

DOMESTIC POOLS

Pool ownership is increasing in this country every year, as it is an amenity the whole family can enjoy, and parents can ensure that their children learn to swim as early as possible. Enthusiastic pool owners maintain that the pool has paid for itself over a couple of years in petrol, club memberships, holidays and entertainment, not to mention better health. A pool setting is ideal for parties for all ages, as everyone becomes much less inhibited near water!

If you are thinking of having a pool, the by-laws of the local authority must be consulted, as, although planning permission may not be necessary for the pool itself, consent may be needed for a plant house and changing room. Questions also might arise about drainage and a water

112

meter. The rateable value may be increased, but this is offset by the increased value of the house. Read all the brochures and compare guarantees and after sales service of well-established firms—still in existence when needed! If it is to be a 'do it yourself' job, obtain information on package deals from the experts, as this might ensure a cheaper job in the long run. If possible visit other privately owned pools in the winter, visit firms' demonstration grounds, or have their representative call.

Pool ownership usually results in the whole family becoming proficient swimmers fairly quickly, and so it must be able to cope with their demands as they grow older. Remember that diving from the side is only safe with a depth of 6' 6". Materials, size, shape, services and extras determine cost, but a purification plant is advisable. Pools can be heated by gas, oil, solar or electricity, the latter 'off peak' in some areas, or even by the central heating system in the house. Heating extends the swimming season and it is very often warmer in than out. Initially extras can be modest, consisting of cleaning apparatus, water testing kit, thermometer and a leaf net. Invariably pool owners make additions over the years so these should be allowed for in the first plan. There should be anchor points in the paving for a pool cover, steps, diving board or chute. Space should be earmarked for plant/storage, changing pavilion, chalet or awning. Electric points for kettle, lights, music, hot plate and barbecue grill, in a future entertainment area, should be connected initially.

A non-slip surround, footbath, lifebuoy or safety line are essential. With very young children a fence round the pool will be necessary, unless it is a free standing pool with removable ladder. The pool needs to be in the maximum sunlight, and if it is to have a diving board it should be sited so that the sun does not shine directly into the diver's eyes.

Protection from gusts of wind, blowing leaves or debris, and drifting snow in winter, is necessary. If the house itself does not provide this shelter, then screening or planting may be needed. Large trees are not good windbreaks as their leaves, fir or pine needles, can foul the water and cause trouble with the plant. A pool sited some distance from the house will mean more costly services, but a pool immediately outside the window is not very attractive in winter.

Each year sees more inflatable, dismountable and lightweight ceiling supports come on to the market. Such pool enclosure can make all the year round swimming possible. With a large house, or out-buildings, an indoor pool is worth considering in our climate! Free standing ones have been fitted into barns, disused squash courts, stable blocks and basements. In the latter suspended ropes, trapeze or rings above the pool surface would provide soft landings for Aquabatics! Always try to see the pool of your choice in use. If money is no object then a custom built pool complete with spot and underwater lighting; sound equipment; with sliding screens to open and close it according to the weather; and beautifully landscaped would make a swimmer's dream.

Reference book:
Build Your Own Swimming Pool, Norman Wills (John Gifford Ltd.).

COMMUNITY EFFORT POOLS

Nowadays people are not prepared to sit back and wait for amenities to be provided by the local council—if it means waiting for years. In small rural communities public spirited committees have set about raising the necessary funds to build a pool. The money has been contributed by every local organization; the schools; generous donations from individuals and firms; and the appropriate grants obtained. The pool has then been maintained by the council for use by schools, clubs, classes and the general public. Co-operation of this kind ensures the best pool possible for the money available, and the fullest use made of it by all concerned, as they rightly look upon it as *their pool*. Such rural pools can benefit the nearby overcrowded town pool, to which rural schools and individuals had to travel.

The phasing of one such pool was open air the first season, diving boards added the second season, and covered over for the third season. When the pool was covered the increased numbers actually learning to swim, the increased proficiency in swimming and diving and the leap in attendance figures, were self evident. The sunbathers and outdoor-spectators were still catered for, as footbaths were built between the lawn and terrace and the sliding glass pool doors, which were opened in summer. The size of a community pool will be determined by cost, and the maximum is usually 25 m. × 12 m. with a depth of 2′ 9″ or 3′ to 6′ 6″ for diving from the side, or 8′ 6″ for a one-metre board. To build this kind of pool, stout hearts and determination are needed on the part of a small band of enthusiasts, when the first flush of keen participation has faded for others.

Reference:
Swimming Pool Review—Design, Construction, Maintenance (Quarterly).
Swimming Pools, Philip H. Perkins (Elsevier)

ORGANIZATION

Once the pool is ready for use, all the hard work and worry entailed will seem well worthwhile. The next stage is to organize its use for the benefit of all concerned. If it is to be used by schools and clubs then good liaison must be established from the outset, to ensure the necessary co-operation and goodwill. Schools will take care of their own pool time-tabling and rule keeping. For clubs I will offer ten TIPS, in the hope that some of them might be helpful:

1. Committee
It is useful to have a bank manager or accountant on the committee. Over and under organization of class and club activities will mean less enjoyment. Some rules will be necessary: a change of shoes on the poolside, hygienic use of footbaths, showers, lavatories and changing rooms *but* it is no use making rules if they cannot be enforced. Various jobs can be shared out according to expertise and interest. An end of season annual meeting, when everything is still fresh in mind, is useful to check progress, plan additional activities, and listen to compliments and complaints! At this meeting the presentation of national awards might also be made: R.L.S.S.; A.S.A.; E.S.S.A. and S.T.A.

2. First Aid
There must be a first-aid kit, access to a telephone, with numbers of doctor and hospital, and addresses of all club members, and transport available. The pool's rescue aids should be close at hand, and a life saver on duty at all sessions. Members of St. John or Red Cross, and a life saver stripped for action, should attend swimming sports. How to give the 'Kiss of Life' must be known, and there should be instruction given in this, and the use of resuscitation equipment. If necessary consult the *Swimming Times* regarding nose clips, ear plugs, eye drops and goggles—the latter for swimmers affected by chlorine. Buy a safety chair.

116

3. Coaches

According to clubs' requirements they should attend local, regional or national courses in swimming, diving, survival, life saving, synchro, water polo, timekeeping, judging, refereeing and examining.

4. Notice boards

Should be eye-catching, regularly changed and kept up to date with posters, leaflets, photographs and news cuttings. In addition there should be reports on the club's progress, details of future TV swimming programmes, new awards, new books and new rules. Cup or sucker hooks for the hanging and easy removal of the Handbooks of the R.L.S.S., A.S.A., E.S.S.A. and *Swimming Times*. A suggestion box could be attached to the board.

5. Apparatus

Consult the *Swimming Times* and *Pool Review* for goods and prices. The store room must be well shelved, and rings can be stored on a long bamboo cane hooked on to the bottom shelf. Alternatively rings can be stored, and easily carried out to the pool, on an upright post fixed to a large base. Stock plenty of spare plugs for rings. Frequent maintenance and renewal of equipment will be necessary, and special checks should be made before sports, or testing for awards.

6. Finance

Respect local feelings, if strongly held, regarding lotteries, football pools, raffles and bingo as the means of raising money. Donations, work cards, brick stamps, mile of pennies, coffee mornings, bring and buy, rummage sales, fêtes and special efforts are a few of the other ways used. A thermometer, graph or notice board, in a central place helps to keep people informed regarding the money needed. Even when the pool is complete there might still be some amenities required such as mirrors, wringer, hair dryer and drink and snack dispensers. Money will be needed for equipment such as rings, floats, rubber bricks, hoops, wall blackboards, stop watch, starting pistol and blocks, racing lanes, water polo ball, loud hailer, 16" battery or electric timing clock. Funds may also be needed to assist talented young swimmers, by free admission and club membership. Help towards the expenses involved in attending courses, and swimming sports might also be necessary in some cases. Clubs might consider transporting handicapped people in the area to their pool. Some clubs have taken handicapped groups abroad to enjoy swimming in a warm and buoyant sea.

7. *Audio/visual aids*

Films, loops and strips can be shown. Before any event check the public address system, record player or tape recorder for amplification. Have a loud hailer and a battery record player in reserve. When possible make a film of the clubs' activities, or take photographs for slides or display, and so record progress by means of a visual record.

8. *Lectures and demonstrations*

Cardboard figures, profile and bird's eye view, jointed with paper clips are easily made, and can be used to illustrate propulsive and recovery movements in swimming, diving and synchro positions. Flannelgraphs are useful in many ways and magnetic boards for water polo. Visiting lecturers must be supplied with all the necessary details. Visiting demonstrators or demonstration teams must know the size and depth of the pool, especially for water polo, synchro and diving. Experts are able and willing to adapt in most cases, but only if given fair warning.

118

9. Publicity

A display showing what the club has achieved is good publicity, and can also be the means of raising money. Typed or duplicated press handouts with organization's name; and name, address and telephone number of person to be contacted for further details. If a press photographer is wanted for an event then plenty of warning should be given. This section can also deal with printing, duplicating, typing, invitations, notices, programmes, lists and reports.

10. Hospitality

For special events there should be catering, adequate reception, sufficient reserved seats and someone to accompany V.I.P.s throughout. If a visitor is to receive a gift choose a steady bearer, as bouquets and baskets of fruit have ended up in many a pool! A gift can be propelled on a float by a swimmer when the poolside is crowded. Ensure that prize winners are able to shake hands and receive their prizes graciously. A towel over the knees is not sufficient protection from chlorinated water which can mark clothing. The whole tone of a club can be made or marred by the courtesy, friendliness and helpfulness shown, or the lack of it.

9 · What Next

Previous chapters have dealt with possible ways of bringing more enjoyment to visits to the pool, and to family, group, club and school sessions. This is, however, only the threshold of enjoyment in, on or under the water. There is a growing range of opportunities for other recreational activities for the swimmer and the choice is open to all.

DISTANCE SWIMMING

When I was young and in my prime,
I swam the channel many a time,
But now I'm wrinkled, old and grey,
I only swim it twice a day.

This rhyme approaches nearer to the truth, as the Channel has now been swum by a fourteen-year-old girl; six times by one man; and by a fifty-five-year-old man, who swam it in both directions in the same year. Non-stop double crossings have been made in just over thirty hours, and the record time for single crossings for both men and women is under ten hours. About a thousand attempts have been made since Captain Webb's success in 1875, and eighty men and thirty-five women have succeeded. Sponsored International Channel Races have been held, and now relay team Channel swimming is becoming very popular. Teams from schools, one with an average age of only twelve years, from clubs, colleges, the services and even a team of handicapped swimmers have been successful. The Channel Swimming Association was formed in 1927 to investigate and authenticate claims, and appoint observers and record details.

Many people get a lot of pleasure out of just swimming up and down a pool for a certain distance, or for a certain time and then getting out. Long swims are used in training for speed and survival swimming, but can become monotonous if only one stroke is used. Alternate lengths of a front and back stroke, or the use of a variety of strokes, including the side stroke and the English back stroke, will enable swimmers to learn which strokes they can call upon in an emergency. The English back stroke correctly performed will help to maintain good posture.

Distance swimming can be used to raise money for a specific purpose. A Channel relay team from Spitalfields market raised £150 for a colleague's widow. A sponsored swim need last only two hours, which is the time most groups are likely to be able to reserve the pool, or it may be a marathon swim. Shrewsbury Swimming Club, for example, raised over £1,500 and the Sub-Aqua Club £190. An announcer kept the spectators informed throughout, and certificates of distances achieved, varying from half a mile to six miles, were provided for swimmers to show their sponsors. The money was given to the Shropshire Spastics' Society for furnishings for the seaside bungalow they had built for severely disabled spastics and their families. In any such swims it must be remembered that a check with the Amateur Swimming Association should be made, so that amateur status is not jeopardized. Such swims are, however, safer than sponsored walks.

The Amateur Swimming Association's Long Distance Championship is still annually held for men and women, over a course of five miles, but no longer in the Thames. The British Long Distance Swimmers' Association record and stage individual and competitive swims in open waters, and hold an International Championship in Lake Windermere. It is possible that a marathon swim may be included

121

in the Olympic Games in the future, as these swims are
staged in many parts of the world.

Reference books

Handbook. British Long Distance Swimmers' Association.
Modern Long Distance Swimming, Commander G. Forsberg
   (Routledge & Kegan Paul).
*Handbook and Rules for Channel Swimming and Relay Team
   Swims*. Channel Swimming Association.

SWIMMING CHAMPIONSHIPS

These are staged for the élite school, club, county and
national competitive swimmers, under the Laws of the
Amateur Swimming Association. Spectators are usually
relatives, friends and the swimming fraternity who appreciate a high standard of performance. Top class and International Championships are frequently featured on TV and
so we can compare stroke techniques, starts, turns and
finishes. We can also note the overall organization, deploy-
ment of officials, and that the slow handclap which accompanies the presentation of awards is traditional and respect-
ful! Those concerned with purchasing pool equipment
should be on the look out for changes in racing lanes,
starting blocks and diving boards, as new pools in Great
Britain, and other countries, are constantly using new
materials and different designs. Unfortunately diving, synchronized swimming and water polo are seen less often on
TV, which means that the general public are not so well
informed about these activities, as about swimming.

SWIMMING GALAS

These can consist of orthodox school or club events, entertaining events for swimmers and spectators alike, or be a mixture of both. A Gala which consists almost entirely of swimmers churning up and down the pool can become very monotonous. The inclusion of some entertaining or instructive display should be timed to give the competitive swimmers a rest, and the spectators and officials a break.

Reference book

Organizing a Swimming Gala—Amateur Swimming Association.

MUSIC AND SWIMMING

Synchronized Swimming consists of performing movements in the water in time to music. It is a competitive sport, which may possibly be included as an event in Olympic Games in the future. In Britain we are just on the threshold, and have much to learn from individuals and teams from America and Canada, but steady progress is now being made.

For well over sixty years 'Scientific Swimming' movements were required for the Award of Merit and Diploma of the Royal Life Saving Society. These are no longer required for the R.L.S.S. awards, but many are included in Synchronized Swimming. This kind of swimming skill has been enjoyed by swimming clubs, too, for many years. Displays combining formation swimming, scientific, alias ornamental, movements and floating figures to whistle cues were given by some clubs. Other clubs performed similarly to a musical accompaniment, and water ballets with special lighting effects were not unknown. American films popularized swimming at that time, with 'Tarzan', Johnny Weismuller, winner of five Olympic Gold Medals, as the star, and there was beautiful swimming in mammoth aqua shows. In

123

1953 another American, Beulah Gundling, visited Britain to demonstrate what superb artistry there was in synchronized swimming.

The Swimming Teachers' Association were the first to introduce synchro into their awards. In 1965 the Amateur Swimming Association formed a National Synchronized Swimming Committee. A film was made, and courses held for coaches, examiners and officials, and a Synchro Award scheme introduced. Gradually the sport spread through clubs, counties and districts, and the first National Competition was held in 1969. The time is now ripe, therefore, for youngsters to find out if Synchro is their particular aquatic medium for enjoyment.

AQUATIC ART

Aquatic Art differs from Synchronized Swimming in that it allows much greater freedom for creativity and self-expression. It is an art form rather than a competitive sport. The International Academy of Aquatic Art holds an annual festival in the U.S.A., for instruction and evaluation of theme-based compositions.

COME DANCING

I was in the open air pool at Scarborough wondering what the Spartans had that I hadn't, when suddenly the organ began to play. We all stopped freezing and were galvanized into action, disporting ourselves in strict tempo, and enjoying it immensely. This reminded me that Ross Eagle taught huge classes of learners to music, in this same pool. In 1933 he was accompanied by the Black Watch Band with 'My Girl's a Yorkshire Girl!' If Synchronized Swimming and Aquatic Art are beyond your expertise, you might either be stimulated by music into learning to swim, or enjoy performing your own modest solo routines to relaxing background music.

A 'Come Dancing' session could be good fun with Old-Time, Latin American, Blues, Beat or the current craze. A song with a local flavour could become the signature tune.

EXAMPLES: 'Bladen Races'; 'She's a Lassie from Lancashire'; ' In Dublin's Fair City'; 'I belong to Glasgow'; 'I love a Lassie'; 'Maybe it's because I'm a Londoner'; 'On Ilkla Moor'; 'Widdicombe Fair'; 'John Peel'; 'Bobbie Shaftoe'; 'The Keel Row'; 'Floral Dance'. Failing a song, a folk dance tune could be used: 'Newcastle'; 'Brighton Camp'; 'Shrewsbury Lasses'; 'Morpeth Rant'; 'Flowers of Edinburgh'; 'Bonnie Dundee'; 'Belfast Reel'; 'All the way to Galway'; 'Cumberland Square'; 'Dorset Triumph'. Foreign dance tunes would add variety and colour to a programme, if chosen for their varied instruments and mood: Israeli; Greek; Spanish; Italian; Hungarian; Russian; Mexican; West Indian; Arabic; Indian.

In the programme there could be a Paul Jones, a Ladies' Choice, a Spot Light Waltz, 'Desert Island Discs' and Square Dancing with the caller, plus microphone, on a diving board. Non-swimmers could join in on the poolside, provided it had a ridge to prevent dirt entering the water, and a suitable surface. Exhibition dances might also be staged on the poolside. Simple demonstrations could be given in the water by a display team. An expert team could use pair linkage in stroke patterns, on the lines of formation dancing teams seen on TV, to a tune like 'Daisy, Daisy'. Vocal groups, decorations and special lighting effects, would all add to the pleasurable atmosphere.

Appropriate music could be played at the beginning of any aquatic event whilst people are being shown to their seats, during intervals, and at the end whilst people are leaving, for example: 'The Eton Boating Song'; 'Skye Boat Song'; 'Old Man River'; 'Volga Boatmen'; 'Blue Danube'; 'Aquarius'. Community singing is possible in some instances: 'Row, row, row your boat'; 'Cruising down the River'; 'Red Sails in the Sunset'; 'Swim Sam Swim'; 'My Bonnie lies over the Ocean'; 'Oh Jemima look at your Uncle Jim'; 'Pedro the Fisherman'; 'I do like to be beside the Seaside'; plus the well-known sea shanties, and appropriate Gilbert and Sullivan songs.

POOL PARTIES

Parties can be held in school's and club's pool sessions, in domestic pools, and at slack times in a hired local pool, or in open waters. The purpose of the party and guests to be invited will dictate the programme, theme and music, as for example: a money raising effort; a social meeting; a children's celebration or fancy dress party. If held in the evening, Japanese lanterns, lighted torches and floating water lily candles make an attractive setting. Those swimming should have their refreshments when they have finished. Care should be taken to ensure that guests do not carry glasses or bottles near to the water, as a breakage will necessitate pool emptying and may damage the plant.

DARKENED POOL

Displays and games can be most effective when only underwater or coloured spot lighting is used. In a public pool such lighting might already be incorporated, even if rarely used. For single occasions only a qualified electrician, using the correct rubber insulated materials, should undertake the job. Cables must be laid well away from seating, entrances and exits, and lighting stands so placed that only the operator can get close to them.

Sequinned or luminous painted costumes—if permitted, coloured or decorated leotards and tights, and decorated caps and masks can be worn. Floating tableaux can be mounted on plywood platforms supported on inner tubes. One suitably costumed and mounted swimmer per float can carry illumination suited to the theme, such as a lighted lantern, or torch fitted into a bamboo cane. The float can be propelled by an unseen partner, if the light is held on the opposite side, and the propelling swimmer wears a long-sleeved leotard, and back paddles with legs beneath the float. The floats can weave in and out, or be propelled in a definite formation, whichever best suits the ability of the propelling swimmers. The music should be chosen to suit the theme: 'Barcarole' for Venetian; steel guitars for Hawaian; flamenco for Gipsy.

Spotlights can be used to fit the choice of music, for instance blue for 'Rhapsody in Blue'. Alternatively the lights can be changed to fit in with the musical phrases. Underwater lighting can be most effective for figure floating and stroke patterns, if it is staged so that the spectators can see what is happening throughout. It will be necessary to experiment with costume colours, to see which show up the best, or the least, for the propelling swimmers.

Underwater torches can be fixed into helmets for swimming on the front or treading water; to polystyrene floats on a waist belt for swimming on the back; or held in the hand and moved in time with slow music. Certain games can be amusing for both swimmers and spectators in a darkened pool. Torch Tag can be played with four carrying lighted underwater torches, and when tagged by other swimmers they hand the torch over. Hunt the Bellman can be played with the bellman having a luminous bell, and the rest wearing luminous eyeless masks. Ball games with a luminous ball or balls can also be played. In an open-air darkened pool a firework display might also be staged, if a check is made with the fire brigade, and all necessary precautions taken.

Reference books

Synchronized Swimming, George Rackham (Faber & Faber Ltd.).

Beulah Gundling's books on Aquatic Art (U.S.A. via the *Swimming Times*).

IN AND OUT

It is very cruel to push, or throw, a nervous person or a non-swimmer into the water, as it might put them off swimming for life. Swimmers should dive or jump in, and not go down the steps.

Old diving boards with a depth of only 6 ft. of water beneath, meant an angled dive or bomb jump. In those days the springboard was little more than a plank of wood covered with slippery matting. With the introduction of a springboard with real spring in it, diving became an acrobatic skill. I well remember my mother returning from the 1924 Paris Olympic Games, thrilled by the performance of the American divers using a springboard with a fulcrum. Progress in springboard and diving-board design has continued with the use of a variety of materials. High-board diving in the past meant outdoor conditions, providing sufficiently deep water, and so the Highgate Diving Club and Jersey Club usually led the field. The possibilities of safe and correct diving are only now being more fully realized in the new pools. The top boards in some pools, formerly used for competitions, are now out of action, either because they are too near the roof, or the water is not deep enough to comply with the present regulations.

Today new public pools usually have 1- and 3-metre springboards, a 5-metre firm board and occasionally a 10-metre board, plus spray nozzles for water disturbance. However, in peak sessions, divers still fare badly, as swimmers are often under the boards, in spite of warning notices. Even when swimmers are asked to keep clear for diving times in each session, novices and divers must queue for turns on the boards. Separate diving sections as in Putney, Coventry and Leeds, or separate diving pools as in Wrexham or Edinburgh, are the answer. The time will surely come when diving, which is allied to gymnastics rather than swimming, will have its own provision. Meanwhile programmed usage for the general public could include safe roped-off sessions for divers, swimmers and non-swimmers. Schools, classes and clubs, with exclusive use of a pool, can plan their diving sessions and coach pupils safely. Anyone who really wants to enjoy diving should seek out a class or club in a pool with the regulation facilities, and a coach.

Chutes were popular in both indoor and outdoor pools in the past, but are now mostly confined to large outdoor lidos. They provide a whole host of ways of getting into the water. Children used to park slides are most inventive on chutes, and their permutations seem endless. Portable fibreglass chutes are now available, which can be used at a right angle, or, where surround space is limited, parallel to the poolside. These could be used in pools of 6 ft. depth under supervision. Many old diving boards are still *in situ* but their use is now forbidden. The possibility of rigging them up with commando netting, rope ladders or ropes could be explored, so that alternative ways of getting in and out are available. They could be no more dangerous than trying to do a

I

vertical dive from an 8-ft. board into a 6-ft. depth, and would be useful for initiative tests and survival training. Temporary erections at least could be made for sports or displays.

I look forward to the day when new pools offer many more alternatives for getting into and out of pools. These might include an inclined trampette; a drop-down trampette; a mono-rail; ropes; a trapeze; rings; parallel ropes across the pool; and arrangements of ropes and rope ladders. Trampolines could be placed in pits with covers, for dry land practice at ground level. This would obviate the storage and erection problems of folding trampolines.

Reference books

Your Book of Diving, Margaret Jarvis (Faber & Faber Ltd.).
Diving, George Rackham (Arco).
Diving; *for Teacher and Pupil*, Rose Mary Dawson (Pelham).
Diving Manual, Amateur Swimming Association.

WATER POLO

Water polo is the only recognized aquatic game, and as such deserves more support. Unfortunately it is rarely seen on TV and so the general public have only a hazy idea of the game. The game has meant a lot to me since the days we wore father's international maroon, blue and green polo caps for charades! Later I played regularly in the Women's Midland League, and against France and Holland, and apart from the odd black eye and kicks in the stomach thoroughly enjoyed it. Gradually the women's game dropped out of favour, largely because, being only a seven-a-side game, the use of pool time for small numbers was more than most clubs could fit into their expanding programmes.

On the mens' side, too, it has had its ups and downs, as in Britain the game had to be played mostly in small pools with a shallow end. In Europe maximum-sized and deeper pitches were used both indoors and in warm seas or rivers, with floating boundaries and nets. This led to the development of a tactically different game, and to see the Hungarians play was sheer joy. However, new pools in Britain are larger and deeper, and have goal posts which fold flat or dismantle easily for storage. In the past polo posts were cumbersome nuisances unless they were hoisted to the roof.

The Amateur Swimming Association in 1970 introduced Bronze, Silver and Gold, Water Polo Proficiency Awards, for both men and women. The taking of these awards should appeal to young club members, and to strong swimmers in schools with their own pools. The money raised from entrance fees will be used for the further development of all aspects of the game. It is hoped that by promoting interest and raising standards we will once again produce major water polo teams in this country.

Young swimmers with the necessary stamina, who enjoy a ball handling game, such as volley ball, basketball and netball, might find that water polo is the game for them. Help could be sought from the nearest good club, service, police or college team. Club, league, county and international matches for seniors, and juniors under eighteen, are played. In 1971 the Amateur Swimming Association inaugurated the Water Polo Boys' Championship for under sixteen club and school teams. Organizers of galas, in large enough new pools, might consider the inclusion of a water polo match in the programme, and so introduce the game to a wider public.

References

Water Polo Rules, Refereeing and Film, Amateur Swimming Association.

All About Water Polo, Kelvin Juba.

How to Play and Teach Water Polo, Charles Hines, U.S.A., (both via the *Swimming Times*).

UNDERWATER

The world under the sea will be more fully exploited in the future, if we can only control its pollution. Future generations may see underwater farming, already pioneered in the Far East, and perhaps, eventually underwater cities. Astronauts have learnt to work underwater as part of their training, and many nations are attempting, for economic and military purposes, to increase the depth to which humans can dive, and the time which can safely be spent underwater.

Underwater exploration brings aesthetic and recreational rewards as well. Rich archaeological finds have already been made in the Mediterranean, where treasures have been recovered from Phoenician and Roman ports. Nearer home, sunken ships of the Armada have been discovered. In the future underwater activities will play a large part in providing the space and opportunities for a wide variety of interests, as rising demand gradually overcrowds existing recreational facilities.

The Spearfishing Club of Great Britain already has its own championship, and sponsors an underwater photography competition. Members of sub-aqua clubs enjoy expeditions, carry out research such as the mapping of seaweed resources, identification of marine life, and exploring pot-holes to discover new entrances, routes and exits.

Artists, designers and architects could perhaps find inspiration in nature's exciting underwater buildings, flora and fauna. A whole new world is waiting, and for the majority of us just to appreciate its wonders would be sufficient.

However, the correct techniques for underwater sport should be learnt under the guidance of an experienced instructor. It is best not to buy equipment without first seeking advice, and the British Sub-Aqua Club will provide information. Initial training is usually given in a pool and progress made from snorkelling to Third, Second and First Class Diver. Membership of a club will ensure the necessary safety precautions, and companionship for coastal and inland water dives. Underwater hockey, with its official rules, and other games are enjoyed as part of the winter training programme. Hockey is a six-a-side game in which a goal is scored by pushing a lead weight along the pool bottom with a concave wooden bat. If there is no club within easy reach a holiday course might be the solution. These are organized by various bodies and vary according to ability. The British Sub-Aqua Club, the Youth Hostel Association, and the Central Council of Physical Recreation can be contacted for details of courses in Britain and abroad. There are even package holidays for sub-aqua exploration of the Red Sea. (*See Plates 6a and b.*)

Reference books

Triton, Journal of the British Sub-Aqua Club.
Underwater Swimming (Know the Game).
Your Book of Underwater Swimming, R. B. Matkin & G. F. Brookes (Faber & Faber Ltd.).
Diving Manual, G. F. Brookes & A. V. Broadhurst (Stanley Paul).
The Last Resource (a study of man's exploitation of the oceans), Tony Loftus (Hamish Hamilton).

ON THE WATER

All kinds of sailing and boating are increasing rapidly in this country, and there is room here to indicate only a few of the recreational fields that are made possible by confidence in and on the water. The growing popularity of outboard motor boats and sailing boats is matched by that of canoeing, rowing, water ski-ing, surf bathing and surf riding. The canals are also gradually being rehabilitated for, or by, the devotees of canal cruising or canoeing. At 4 m.p.h. with easy moorings, and averaging four boats per mile the canals are relaxing, even though there are still locks! In contrast there is now the water scooter, which could be a means of faster transport by water, a leisure craft, or be used for racing or water games. Snow-mobiles are now used by Laplanders, and as an alternative to ski-ing in many parts of the world, and there is far more water than snow! Mini-hovercrafts and water fun cars might well provide the water enjoyment of the go-karting and motor-cycling fraternities. Swimming, however, must always be the passport. Statistics show that fishermen, whether in boats, standing in waders, or even only beside water, must be able to swim. (*See* page 32.)

Appendix I · Prizes

Prizes are not usually awarded at 'fun and games' sports, but if they are to be awarded for the more orthodox events then they should be suitable for the age and sex of the competitors. These entrants must also have their amateur status protected, which rules out: money, saving certificates, orders for goods, food, consumable goods and clothes, as distinct from swimming costume, training suit, or tie.

If cups are chosen try to obtain either plinthless ones, or those with the cup and plinth joined. Some handicapped and very young swimmers find it extremely difficult to shake hands and receive a cup on a plinth. Previous practice will ensure a gracious instead of a hazardous reception. Medals tend to sit in boxes and collect dust, as they do not display easily. Certificates display much better, and a keen youngster can save on wallpaper with them! However, he will not want to do this if they insult his expertise and intelligence, which can happen when a large supply of certificates is bought and becomes outdated. I have seen certificates in which the diver, weighed down by an old-fashioned costume, stands a yard from the edge of the board with palms together, no doubt saying a necessary prayer! Others have depicted out of date life-saving land drill and resuscitation methods. Badges are popular, especially with children, but choose good-quality ones which will wash, and be chlorine and sea proof if for a swimming costume, and will dry clean if for a blazer or training suit.

Books, but not tokens, on swimming, diving, synchro, sub-aqua and water polo are obviously apt, as are handbooks, the *Swimmers Diary*, the *E.S.S.A. School Swimmer* or a *Swimming Times* subscription. The range of prizes might well be widened to include other suitable books, and the local children's librarian and reference librarian could be consulted. Records, but not tokens, of popular or classical music which centre around the sea, water and swimming could also be considered, and the local record librarian would advise. Reproductions of suitable famous paintings could be obtained from The National Gallery, London.

There are numerous other possibilities, linked with water, which could be awarded as prizes: photograph, news cuttings, autograph and stamp albums, with the club's book plate inside; swimming stamps; kits for ship building; sea shells—for a ladies' event large ones suitable for floral decoration; ship in a bottle; Little Mermaid in Copenhagen china; aquaria; stop watch; bag for swimming kit; swimming kit; club badge or tie; swimming log book. If in doubt consult the swimmers as they will at least know what they do not want. When I was competing the appropriate prize always seemed to be fish knives and forks!

BOOKS
with Club Book Plate inside

Wind in the Willows	Kenneth Grahame
Alice in Wonderland	Lewis Carrol
The Water Babies	Charles Kingsley
Tom Sawyer	Mark Twain
The Sea Egg	L. M. Boston
The Magic Squid	R. Manning-Sanders
A Book of Mermaids	R. Manning-Sanders
The Sea Friends	P. Ropner
Plan for Birdsmarsh	K. M. Peyton
Small Boat Adventures	M. Brown
Tarka the Otter	H. Williamson
Seal Morning	Rowena Farre

BOOKS

The Water Gipsies	A. P. Herbert
Hornblower Series	C. S. Forester
A Ring of Bright Water	Gavin Maxwell
Three Men in a Boat	Jerome K. Jerome
The Cruel Sea	Nicholas Monsarrat
The Kon Tiki Expedition	Thor Heyerdahl
The Sea around Us	Rachel Carson
The Big Fisherman	Lloyd C. Douglas
World without Sun etc.	Jacques Cousteau

RECORDS
with Club Book Plate on sleeve

Fingals Cave	Mendelssohn
Calm Sea and Prosperous Voyage	Mendelssohn
Water Music	Handel
Flying Dutchman	Wagner
Swan Lake	Tchaikovsky
Tuonela	Sibelius
La Mer	Debussy
Carnival of Animals (The Swan)	Saint-Saens
Pearl Fishers (Extracts from Opera)	Bizet
The Gondoliers (Extracts from Opera)	Gilbert and Sullivan
H.M.S. Pinafore (Extracts from Opera)	Gilbert and Sullivan
Pirates of Penzance (Extracts from Opera)	Gilbert and Sullivan
Peter Grimes (Extracts from Opera)	Benjamin Britten
Sea Pictures	Elgar
Summer Night on the River	Delius
Fantasia on British Sea Songs	Henry Wood
Sea Symphony	Vaughan Williams
Façade (The Hornpipe)	William Walton
The Planets (Venus; Neptune)	Gustav Holst
'Full fathom five thy father lies: Of his bones are coral made; Those are pearls that were his eyes:'	Shakespeare – setting by Robert Johnson

K
137

PAINTINGS, Etc.
with Club Book Plate on back

Peter getting out of Nick's Pool	David Hockney, Walker Art Gallery, Liverpool
Swimming Race	Diana Cummings, Walker Art Gallery, Liverpool
The Mermaid	C. N. Kennedy, Leeds Art Gallery
The Bathers	H. S. Tuke, Leeds Art Gallery
August Blue	H. S. Tuke, Tate Gallery
The Mermaids Book	E. Matthew Hale, Tate Gallery
Cradle Rock, Guernsey	Pierre Renoir, Tate Gallery
La Baignade	Georges Seurat, Tate Gallery
Snowstorm at Sea	J. M. W. Turner, Tate Gallery
A Summer Day	William Scott, Manchester Corporation
Noonday	William Scott, Manchester Corporation
Willows by a stream, etc.	John Constable, Victoria & Albert Museum
Water-lilies, etc.	Claude Monet, National Gallery
Birth of Venus	Botticelli, reproductions from shops
The Aqueduct	Paul Cezanne, reproductions from shops
Fish Magic	Paul Klee, reproductions from shops
Still Life with Goldfish	Henri Matisse, reproductions from shops
Women on the Shore	Henri Matisse, reproductions from shops
The Moat	Paul Nash, reproductions from shops
The Pool	Paul Nash, reproductions from shops

Plus paintings by: Andre Derain, Raoul Dufy, Paul Gaughin, Oskar Kokoschka, Albert Marquet, Stanley Spencer, Christopher Wood, etc. (Consult art books in libraries or shops.)

A carp in a pool (Japanese woodcut), Katsushika Taito, Victoria & Albert Museum

Hollow of the deep sea wave (Japanese woodcut), Hokusai, Victoria & Albert Museum

The Waterfall of Yoro (Japanese woodcut), Hokusai, British Museum

Spirit of the Waves (Chinese painting on silk), Hsuan, British Museum

The Neptune Dish (Roman silver Mildenhall Treasure), British Museum

Appendix II · Addresses

ROYAL LIFE SAVING
   SOCIETY
Chief Secretary,
14 Devonshire Street,
Portland Place,
London, W1N 2AT.

SURF LIFE SAVING
   ASSOCIATION
Hon. Secretary,
10 Porthmeor Square,
St. Ives,
Cornwall.

ROYAL SOCIETY FOR THE
   PREVENTION OF
   ACCIDENTS
52 Grosvenor Gardens,
London, S.W.1.

THE ASSOCIATION OF
   SWIMMING THERAPY
James McMillan,
22 Arnos Road,
London, N.11.

ST. JOHN AMBULANCE
   ASSOCIATION
10 Grosvenor Crescent,
London, S.W.1.

BRITISH RED CROSS
   SOCIETY
14–15 Grosvenor Crescent,
London, S.W.1.

AMATEUR SWIMMING
   ASSOCIATION
N. W. Sarsfield, Secretary,
314 Grays Inn Road,
London, W.C.1.

A.S.A. AWARDS SECRETARY
Miss L. V. Cook,
12 Kings Avenue,
Woodford Green,
Essex.

A.S.A. SWIMMERS' DIARY
H. Cottle,
5 West View,
Sacriston,
Durham.

A.S.A. APPROVED CHARTS
Bovril Ltd.,
Southbury Road,
Enfield,
Middlesex.

SWIMMING TEACHERS' ASSOCIATION
Ray Clements,
National Hon. Secretary,
1 Birmingham Road,
West Bromwich,
Staffs.

BRITISH COACHES' ASSOCIATION
George Ball,
Hon. Secretary,
26 Whitby Avenue,
Fartown,
Huddersfield, Yorks.

ENGLISH SCHOOLS' SWIMMING ASSOCIATION
E. H. Burden,
Hon. General Secretary,
190 Nether Street,
West Finchley,
London, N.3.

E.S.S.A. TEACHING SWIMMING BATH SCHEME
Jack Warrick,
Hon. Secretary,
47 Woodhall Gate,
Pinner,
Middlesex.

THE INSTITUTE OF BATHS MANAGEMENT
256A Green Lanes,
Palmers Green,
London, N.13.

'SWIMMING POOL REVIEW'
Armour House,
Bridge Street,
Guildford, Surrey.

BRITISH LONG DISTANCE SWIMMERS' ASSOCIATION
J. Robinson,
Hon. Secretary,
45 Melrose Avenue,
Billingham,
Durham.

CHANNEL SWIMMING ASSOCIATION
John Floydd,
Hon. Secretary,
8 Manor Road,
Folkestone,
Kent.

BRITISH SUB-AQUA CLUB
160 Great Portland Street,
London, W.1.

COMMITTEE NAUTICAL ARCHAEOLOGY
Miss J. du Plat Taylor,
Secretary,
Institute of Archaeology,
31 Gordon Square,
London, W.C.1.

'THE SWIMMING TIMES'
Kelvin Juba, Editor,
Acorn House,
314 Grays Inn Road,
London, W.C.1.

NISSEN TRAMPOLINE CO.
    LTD.
Tallon Road,
Hutton,
Brentwood, Essex.

EN-TOUT-CAS LTD.
(Swimming Aids),
Syston,
Leicester, LE7 8NP.

'WHICH'
Consumers' Association,
Caxton Hill,
Hertford.

CENTRAL COUNCIL OF
    PHYSICAL RECREATION
26 Park Crescent,
London, W1N 4AJ.

STUDIO MARGARET
    AQUATOGS
(Hire of old-fashioned bathing
    costumes)
32 Victoria Road,
Wisbech, S.

NATIONAL GALLERY
    PUBLICATIONS DEPT.
Trafalgar Square,
London, W.C.2.

DEPT. OF EDUCATION
    AND SCIENCE
Curzon Street,
London, W.1.

CONCLUSION

When the pollution problem is solved we must hope that swimmers will again enjoy:

WATER

'Nothing is lovelier than moving water,
The diamond element, innumerable jewel,
Brittle and splintering under the sharp sun,
Yet softer than doves' feathers, and more smooth
Than down of swan.

Nothing is lovelier than water lying still,
When the Moon takes the stillness for her glass.'

GERALD BULLETT, *Poems in Pencil*, 1937
(published by J. M. Dent)

Index

Compiled by Terence Miller

Page numbers in **bold** type are more important references. *Italic numbers* refer to plates.